The British Isles

First published in Great Britain 1978 by Colour Library International Ltd.
© Illustrations: Colour Library International.
Colour Separations by La Cromolito, Milan, Italy.
Display and text filmsetting by Focus Photoset, London, England.
Printed and bound by L.E.G.O. Vicenza, Italy.
All rights reserved.
ISBN 0-8317-1000-4
MAYFLOWER BOOKS

The British Isles

914.2

Produced by
TED SMART & DAVID GIBBON

MAYFLOWER BOOKS, INC.,
NEW YORK 10022.

London

London was founded in A.D. 43 by the Romans who named it Londinium. The site they chose, on the banks of the River Thames, proved the most suitable in a number of respects. It held the best position for building a bridge and it was the farthest point upstream navigable by ships from the continent. The two gravel hills, known today as Cornhill and Ludgate Hill, provided strong defence positions and the fertile land for farming, and the abundance of timber, made it an ideal site on which to build.

After this early settlement was sacked by Boadicea, Queen of the Iceni, the Romans built a strong wall for protection against further attacks, thus creating the area we know as the city. They also built a fine network of roads extending to all parts of the country, and having a strategic position opposite Europe, Londinium soon became a significant trading centre. Today London is an important centre of finance and commerce, three of the most notable buildings being the Bank of England, the Stock Exchange and Lloyds.

Just to the east of the city is the Tower of London, one of the capital's most impressive and most visited buildings. Built of stone from Normandy, the Tower was begun by William the Conquerer shortly after 1066 but was not completed for several centuries. At one time it was the Royal Mint, and it was also once the site of the execution block. Famous figures of history, the ill-fated Anne Boleyn and Lady Jane Grey to name but two, lost their heads here, and many were imprisoned in the dungeons. This secure building today houses the magnificent Crown Jewels and a large collection of armour, spears and arrows.

From the time of the Norman Conquest, London's growth has been irregular. Large numbers of people died of the Black Death, the name given to the bubonic plague which spread from China and was rampant throughout Europe from the 14th century. The worst outbreak in London was in 1665, the year before the Great Fire which destroyed so much of the prosperous capital.

The fire started in a baker's oven in Pudding Lane. Buildings at that time were still built mainly of wood and were very close together, and fanned by strong winds the fire spread rapidly. Altogether over 13,000 buildings were destroyed, but fortunately there was remarkably little loss of life. Thereafter, rebuilding was in brick or stone and the eminent architect, Sir Christopher Wren, was engaged to design amongst other buildings a new St Paul's Cathedral and several city churches.

Part of the restoration work resulted in the creation of London's many beautiful squares which today provide welcome relief from the noise of traffic and bustle of the streets. Many of the lovely parks such as St James' Park, Hyde Park and Regent's Park which were formerly royal hunting grounds, became public, and Londoners and visitors alike may now spend a pleasant few hours walking and relaxing in the picturesque, peaceful gardens.

The Victorians, anxious to promote the arts and sciences, were responsible for the Royal Albert Hall and numerous imposing museums, many of which were financed from the profits of the Great Exhibition of 1851. London's skyline, transformed by the Victorian buildings, was largely destroyed in World War II and in their place are now many tall, modern office and apartment blocks which, though they may lack the charm of the older buildings, are considered more suited to twentieth century living.

The Industrial Revolution and the subsequent development of the railways were important factors contributing to the rapid growth of London's suburbs, making it today one of the world's largest cities both in area and population.

For centuries London has occupied a prime position not only as the capital of England and the seat of government, but also as a centre for the arts: a major tourist attraction of the city.

One of the favourite areas for visitors is Westminster. The distinctive buildings grew up around the beautiful Gothic Abbey which was built on a marshy site that was once known as Thorney Island. The majority of England's sovereigns were crowned in the Abbey and many, too, have been buried here, together with others who have left their mark on English history: statesmen, writers and the famous 'unknown warrior'.

Alongside Westminster are the ornate and rambling buildings of the Houses of Parliament, officially known as the New Palace of Westminster. The Old Palace was almost entirely destroyed by fire in 1834 and just over 100 years later, during World War II, the House of Commons was partly destroyed in an air raid. When restoration work was carried out at the end of the war its unique character was, however, preserved. The famous clock tower by the House of Commons is known for its large bell, Big Ben, so named after the first Commissioner of Works, Sir Benjamin Hall. In the tower are also cells, where Members of Parliament can be confined for a breach of Parliamentary privilege. It is interesting to note that they have not been used since 1880.

The administrative centre of the whole country is based in Whitehall, a gracious thoroughfare lined with many government offices. Downing Street, in which is situated the Prime Minister's residence, is a short distance away, and close by is Buckingham Palace, with its unforgettable classical facade, the principal home of the reigning monarch since the time of Queen Victoria.

The West End of London is the area known for its shops and nightlife. Oxford Street, Regent Street and Bond Street are three of the most famous streets of London, lined with beautiful shops, many selling exclusive goods. A variety of entertainment is offered in the West End, from the night clubs of Soho to the fine arts. London is the home of some of the finest theatres in the world, producing a wide range of plays and musicals. Ballet and opera are frequently performed and a classical concert in one of London's beautiful concert halls can be heard every night. Fine collections of art are on show in the elegant galleries of London, and there are always exhibitions to visit on a variety of subjects. The many cinemas, always popular, show the very latest films. For the sporting enthusiast, the venues in the suburbs of Wimbledon, Wembley and Crystal Palace offer the very best facilities for both watching and playing many popular sports. With its pageants and ceremonies, monuments and stately homes to visit, London is indeed a city with much to offer to suit every taste and interest.

Left. Big Ben's clock tower.

Overleaf. A selection of the colour, excitement and pageantry that are to be seen in London.

ndon's size can be
rwhelming for visitors
d it keeps growing.
e suburbs reach for
es out into the
rounding countryside.
vertheless, there are
plenty of parks,
prisingly large in area, in
centre of London –
asant oases of green
ce, in which it is easy
orget that this is the
rt of one of the world's
at cities. London has a
lth of interesting
dings to see, most of
m historic and some of
m new.

beautiful dome of
en's masterpiece – St.
l's Cathedral – is
wn *left* and it contrasts
dly with a modern
terpiece *above* , the
ring Post Office Tower.
sts on any visitor's list
surely the Queen's
don home,
kingham Palace *top*
t, the magnificent
ery of the Houses of
liament and the clock
er of Big Ben seen
across the River
mes *right*, the famous
t Street with St. Paul's
hedral *centre right* and
ory-enriched
liament Square
leaf.

11

Trafalgar Square *left below right* with its beautiful fountains, Nelson's column and hordes of ever-hungr pigeons is a favourite meeting place for visi from all over the wor The square was laid commemorate Lord Nelson's famous nava victory of 1805.

At the top of the Post Office's 620 ft. high telecommunications tower *below* there is revolving restaurant providing remarkabl views of London.

Although it no longer dominates London, a architect Sir Christo Wren intended it sho St. Paul's Cathedral, *above right* from Waterloo Bridge, stil excites the imaginati

14

16

rial views of a city always lend an
citing new aspect to it. Buildings,
eets, rivers and parks that are
niliar sights from eye-level are seen
heir relationship to one another
t is impossible to see in any other
y.

e aerial photographs on these pages
w the Tower of London, Tower
dge and St. Catherine's Dock *left*
left, the Houses of Parliament,
stminster Abbey and the Vickers
ver *top centre and top right*, HMS
fast and the Tower of London
ove and the impressive sight of St.
l's Cathedral and the City *right*.

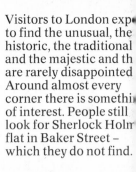

Visitors to London expect
to find the unusual, the
historic, the traditional
and the majestic and they
are rarely disappointed.
Around almost every
corner there is something
of interest. People still
look for Sherlock Holmes'
flat in Baker Street –
which they do not find.

There is, however, a
Sherlock Holmes pub
centre left named after the
great man.

A yacht marina *top left*
nestles almost under the
shadow of the Tower.

Buckingham Palace
bottom left has been the
sovereign's London home
since the time of Queen
Victoria. The picture *top*
was taken at Sandringham,
the Queen's estate in
Norfolk. Outside
Buckingham Palace
stands the Victoria
Memorial and it was here
that the photograph
above of one of the
winged figures was taken.

18

The origins of the Tower
of London *top right and below* date back to
William the Conqueror.
It attracts visitors for many reasons: its historic
associations, the Crown Jewels housed within and
the spectacle of the Yeoman Warders *above and bottom right* as they
go about their duties in their colourful costumes.

There can be few more impressive sights than
Tower Bridge, particularly when seen against the
setting sun *right*.

19

REGIONS CÆSAR NEVER KNEW
THY POSTERITY SHALL SWAY

Subway

ght transforms the city.
odlighting accentuates
tures that might pass
ost unnoticed during
e day; neon signs flash
eir messages, fountains
rkle and water reflects
e soft glow of the
ildings above its
ttering surface. The
e when all this is seen
best advantage is when
s not yet quite dark –
en there is a faint glow
the sky against which
e silhouettes of
ildings can still be seen.

e House of Commons'
ck tower *left* is named
er its bell, Big Ben, and
e whole structure is
own by this name
oughout the world. The
tue in the foreground is
t of Boadicea, an
cient chieftainess.

ristmas decorations in
gent Street *above*.

right The
mistakable shape of the
uses of Parliament
h Lambeth Bridge in
foreground.

e brashness of
cadilly Circus is shown
t, contrasting with the
gance of Trafalgar
uare *centre right* and
rleaf.

Each summer, the famo
Promenade Concerts a
held in the equally fam
Royal Albert Hall *left*
which has also been the
venue for such diverse
entertainments as pop
concerts and boxing.

Horse Guards, in
Whitehall, is a favourit
with tourists, who
particularly enjoy seein
the splendidly turned o
mounted guards *below.*

Pictured *bottom left* ar
the Royal Exchange an
the Bank of England, in
the City.

No 10 Downing Street
right is the official
residence of the Prime
Minister, the highest
elected office in the lan
A rather unimposing
building from the outsi
it has a considerably
larger interior than mi
be imagined and it has
been the setting for
meetings and decisions
that have affected the l
of many thousands of
people, in peace and w

The lovely stained-glass window *above* in the Royal Air Force Memorial Chapel in Westminster Abbey *top right* commemorates the airmen who lost their lives in the Battle of Britain.

The Law Courts *right* are situated just outside the boundaries of the City of London.

...ents in history, some-
...nes insignificant in
...emselves, are usually
...e basis of traditions
...at grow through the
...ars and become part of
...e accepted ceremonies
...at colour the life of the
...pital. The ceremonies,
...ch as Changing the
...uard at Buckingham
...lace, Mounting the
...uard at Horse Guards
...rade, Gun Salutes to
...ark important
...niversaries, and
...obably the most
...pressive spectacle of
..., the ceremony of
...oping the Colour,
...ich marks the
...ueen's official birthday
...d is held on Horse
...uards Parade in June
...ch year, all draw huge
...owds of people.

England

Compared to Scotland and Wales, England is a gentle, low-lying country and, on the geological time scale, relatively young. The earliest men to inhabit the country made little impression on it and left behind them only their makeshift tools and their bones. They hunted animals, fished the seas and rivers and lived in caves. As time passed, their way of life was replaced by that of Stone Age men, who were the first farmers, tending sheep and cattle and growing barley and wheat. Gradually, skills developed, such as working in bronze and iron. This was the era of Stonehenge, that mammoth undertaking on Salisbury Plain that still astounds archaeologists of the 20th century.

A.D. 43 brought the Romans to Britain, and with them came the advanced knowledge of their great Empire. Their influence on the countryside and the people was profound and was to last for four hundred years. Long, straight roads like Fosse Way and Watling Street, camps at Chester and towns such as London and Bath demonstrated their more advanced way of life and their skills. What is now St Albans was chosen as the site of Verulanium, an important Roman town. It is believed that it was a municipium – in which the inhabitants had the same rights as the citizens of Rome. Today a hypocaust – a heating system – and a theatre can still be seen, in addition to many other relics of that time.

Following the withdrawal of the Romans in 407 the Germanic Angles and Saxons overran the whole of England except for Cornwall and Cumberland. Some time later the Danes invaded and for a short period England was ruled by Danish kings. The conquest of Britain by the Normans in 1066 was the last successful military invasion of the country. They built massive strongholds, such as the keep of the Tower of London, new Abbeys and churches – of which St Mary's, at Iffley in Oxfordshire is a fine example – and established great Baronial estates. Eighty forests were set aside for hunting and were ruled by strict laws. William the Conqueror was responsible for clearing away much of the ancient woodland of the New Forest and in so doing destroyed many Saxon villages. Commoners were allowed to graze their animals in the forest for no more than five months each year and to be caught killing a deer meant certain death for the poacher.

French and Latin elements of the Norman's language combined with the Germanic, Celtic and Danish tongues of the old inhabitants to create a common language which is still regarded as a very complex one, with many regional dialects. The physical characteristics of all the invaders who came to these shores may still be seen in the diverse range of features of today's people.

In the Middle Ages England experienced wars, a strong monarchy and the devastating Black Death – a plague that accounted for a large proportion of the country's inhabitants. Later, under the Tudors, England began to trade with Russia, Turkey and, eventually, India. From the late 18th century the whole country developed rapidly with the Industrial Revolution, which created an organized industrial working class. The steam engine was invented and factories and mills became a familiar part of the landscape. In the 20th century, as technology has become more complex, promising awe-inspiring advancement in the future, so English people have become more aware of their long and rich history.

The English countryside has always been appreciated, particularly for its great variety of scenery. Lakes, set like jewels amongst the magnificent Cumbrian mountains of the Lake District, contrast with the extensive, flat farmland of East Anglia, where wheat and spring flowers ripen to perfection in the long hours of sunshine and relatively low rainfall.

In the Midlands, the industrial heart of the country, vast factories produce cars and plastics, pottery and porcelain. It is hard to realise that only one hundred miles to the southeast is Kent, the 'garden' of England, which excels in the growing of apples and strawberries, plums and hops.

Picturesque fishing villages, idyllic sandy bays and a mild climate give rise to a thriving holiday trade in the counties of Devon and Cornwall – but it is a world apart from the great fishing ports of Hull and Grimsby, or the huge chemical works and noisy shipyards of the north-east.

Pretty, yellowstone Cotswold villages provide a feeling of tranquillity rarely experienced in the bustling cities of London or Liverpool, Manchester or Birmingham, where multi-storey blocks are replacing blackened, Victorian slums, reminders of the Industrial Revolution. And yet these same grimy old buildings have their place in the country's heritage and they have provided the inspiration for many English painters, notably L. S. Lowry, who found in these often dingy scenes an air of unreality and a strange beauty. Such scenes did not exist, of course, in the days of Gainsborough or Constable who recorded, and interpreted, so superbly the landscapes of Suffolk. Today, many of the churches, mills, meadows and farms that they saw and painted remain largely untouched, or seemingly so, by the passing of time.

Time seems to have had little effect on the attractive islands around England's shores. The Isle of Man, set in the middle of the Irish Sea, is one of the smallest independent sovereign countries under the Crown. Ruled by a Lieutenant Governor, it has its own parliament, the Tynwald, and its own laws and taxes. Island towns, such as Ramsey and Douglas, are also popular holiday resorts and the island attracts many thousands of motor-cycle enthusiasts to the annual T.T. races, which take part on the island's roads.

Adopted by the Victorians as a holiday island, the Isle of Wight is separated from the mainland by the Solent. In summer it is extremely popular with holidaymakers taking advantage of the sandy beaches and lovely surrounding countryside.

Farther south, beyond Land's End, are the delightful Isles of Scilly, reached by boat or helicopter from Penzance. The mild climate facilitates the growth of early flowers and vegetables which, together with tourism, are important sources of income.

Almost every town, city and village in England has something to offer the native or visitor alike, and the surrounding countryside provides rich and varied landscapes that can be enjoyed afresh with every changing season.

Left. The dramatic chalk cliffs known as the Seven Sisters, in Sussex.

Polperro, Cornwall, *abo* lies in a sheltered inlet between two headlands. one of the most popular Cornwall's many attract villages.

Longships Lighthouse *le* the south-west tip of England. Beyond the lighthouse lie the Isles o Scilly. The coast in this a is noted for its rugged beauty.

From slightly farther alc the coast the setting of Polperro *above right* ca clearly be seen. The hou overlook the welcome haven of the harbour.

Looe *right* is a delightfu holiday centre in a beau county. It is situated on banks of the Looe river has a very individual ch

Overleaf. Lagan Rock a Treen Cliff, Cornwall.

30

134

tagel is a Cornish
stal village *left* with
ong legendary
nections with King
hur and it is believed
t the great King built a
tle here predating the
sent one.

e of the most famous of
nwall's many
turesque holiday
orts is the erstwhile
ple fishing village of
vagissey *below left*.

tured *below* is Cape
nwall, which lies near
ust, the most westerly
n in England.

e westernmost point of
mainland of England
at the appropriately
ned Land's End *right*,
matic, moody and with
ospheric granite cliffs
nging into the sea.

oe *centre right* is
isual in that it is clearly
ided by its river and
ced by a Victorian
lge. The two parts of
very popular resort on
south Cornish coast
known as West Looe
East Looe respectively.

e hard stone known as
pentine was once
rried near Cadgwith
it and an old water-
eel, which was used to
ve machinery when the
nes were in operation,
y still be seen near the
age.

Dartmouth, Devon *left*
pictured from Kingswear
As its name implies,
Dartmouth lies at the m[...]
of the River Dart and it i[...]
the home of the Royal N[...]
College. Dartmouth's inr[...]
harbour is shown *centre*
left.

Clovelly *below* is a
fascinating village that
consists of a single, steep
street of steps that desce[...]
for 400 feet to the pebble
beach and tiny quay.

Sidmouth *bottom left* is [...]
seaside resort and marke[...]
town that lies south-east [...]
Exeter. This particular
picture shows the beach
and the so-called Jacob's
Ladder.

The village of Lynmou[...]
above right overlooks th[...]
wide sweep of Lynmout[...]
Bay. It lies on the edge o[...]
the beautiful countrysid[...]
Exmoor, where the East
and West Lyn Rivers joi[...]
the sea.

Cockington, *right* a quai[...]
little village west of
Torquay, attracts many
visitors. It is famous for [...]
thatched cottages and fo[...]
the old forge, which is st[...]
in working order.

Teignmouth, *overleaf* is [...]
resort at the mouth of th[...]
River Teign.

36

The coasts of Devon, b
north and south, attrac
many thousands of visi
each year, which is hard
surprising in view of th
beautiful scenery,
fascinating fishing villa
and splendid resorts tha
the county has to offer.
Salcombe *top left* is
Devon's most southerly
resort and a noted yach
centre. Brixham *right* o
housed one of the most
prosperous fishing flee
the west of England. It i
also famed as the landir
place of William of Ora
in 1688, an event that w
the turning-point in the
'Glorious Revolution'.

It is not only the coasts
attract tourists to glori
Devon, however. Inlan
scenery is equally beau
and there are many
interesting and lovely
places to visit, such as
Bampton *far left*, *centr*
where an annual pony f
is held in October,
Buckland-in-the-Moor
centre, which must be c
of the most photograph
villages in England,
Widecombe-in-the-Mo
high on Dartmoor *belo*
and the magnificent Ch
Chancel of Exeter
Cathedral *below right*.

The very ground on wh
the ruins of Glastonbu
Abbey Somerset, *left* st
seem steeped in legend
is believed to be the sit
the first Christian chur
in Britain, and it is said
that King Arthur was
buried here.

Wells Cathedral *below*
begun in the 12th centu
and completed in the 1
Its west front is consid
to be one of the finest i
Britain.

Visitors, including
architectural students,
come from many lands
see Bath, not only for it
Abbey *right* but also fo
superb architecture
bottom left, as it is the
finest intact example of
Georgian city in Britai

On the coast road that
skirts Exmoor there are
many lovely villages, so
many in fact that it is
almost impossible to
choose between them.
Driving along this road
however, it is extremel
difficult to resist stoppi
to look at the old pack-
horse bridge *centre left*
Allerford. The setting i
exactly right and, if the
weather is kind, the sce
epitomises this particul
part of the countryside

42

Although the exterior o
Wells Cathedral *above*
very impressive, it is the
interior that provides so
quite breathtaking exam
of the stonemason's cra
Also housed here is an
excellent example of an
astronomical clock whi
dates from 1392.

The City of Bath, deligh
situated on the winding
Avon, was originally a
Roman settlement. Rob
Adams designed Pulten
Bridge *left* which is a u
example of the charm f
which the city is noted.

Bath Spa is famous for i
Roman remains. The m
outstanding of these is
undoubtedly the Roma
Baths *right*.

Gloucester Cathedral *le*
has been described as the
sixth most beautiful
building in Europe. The
magnificent reredos of
high altar was designed
by Sir Gilbert Scott.

Below is the Norman
tower of Tewkesbury
Abbey seen from across
the river. Tewkesbury w
the site of a Yorkist
victory in the Wars of th
Roses in 1471.

The area of England tha
we know as the Cotswo
is one of winding roads
and mellow stone house
It was once the centre o
the wool industry and th
wool merchants built
many of the lovely
churches and manor
houses that delight us
today. *Right.* The sleepy
village of Upper Slaugh
pictured in the early
morning not far from
Naunton *below right.*

The Avon Gorge is
spanned by Brunel's
Clifton Suspension Brid
centre left of 1864. Rath
more recent, but equally
graceful, is the Severn
Suspension Bridge *left*
which was opened in 19
providing a link betwee
England and Wales acro
the river estuary.

46

the crags of Symonds
in Hereford and
rcester stand the ruins
Goodrich Castle, which
to the troops of Oliver
omwell during the Civil
r. Ross on Wye and the
er Wye is pictured
ove left, and *left* is a
w of the River Wye
m Yat Rock. A
ightful view of the
n of Ross on Wye,
ich dates from Roman
es is shown *right.*

e Old House, Hereford,
ictured *far left* and the
nquil mood of summer
aptured *above* in the
light and shadow of
urch Lane, Ledbury.

49

Worcester's magnificent cathedral *right and bottom left* dominates the ancient city. The cathedral was begun in 1084 and building continued until the 14th century. It contains the tomb of the notorious King John. The city stands on the banks of the River Severn, in the centre of rich agricultural land. Worcester is world famous for its porcelain and one of the finest collections of Worcester porcelain and bone china may be seen in the city's Dyson Perrins Museum.

The Vale of Evesham is noted for its fruit-growing industry and the centre of this industry is Evesham itself. It is an elegant market town with two notable churches *top left* All Saints – parts of which date from the 12th century – and St. Lawrence's.

The picture *centre left* was taken at the village of Charlton, not far from Evesham.

Visitors have enjoyed the mellow beauty of Broadway for about a hundred years. It is regarded by many as the perfect example of a Cotswold village and, indeed, was once known as the 'Painted Lady of the Cotswolds'. Even today, a walk around the village, *left* despite the trappings of modernity, the inevitable cars and television aerials, gives a feeling of stepping back into a more leisurely age *near left bottom*.

The origin and purpose of the
giant prehistoric stone circles of
Stonehenge, Wiltshire *above and
bottom right* are still the subject
of debate and speculation. The
stones themselves are believed to
have been brought from
Pembrokeshire, in Wales and each
of the large stones weighs some
twenty-six tons. Whatever their
original purpose, the stones
remain an enigmatic and
fascinating monument.

The spire of Salisbury Cathedral
left, the highest in England, rises
from the "water meadows" of the
Avon with undiminished impact
from different viewpoints. The
cathedral dates from 1220, and it
has a dial-less clock dating from
1326. The cathedral library
contains one of the four copies of
the Magna Carta.

Castle Combe *above right* is
recognized as one of the prettiest
villages in England. It is set in a
lovely valley, and its old Market
Cross still survives, adding a
timeless air to this pleasant
corner of Wiltshire.

ound the village of
ebury, in Wiltshire, is
e of Britain's most
portant prehistoric
numents, the
ebury Stone Circle
ove left. This circle pre-
es the main parts of
nehenge by some 200
rs.

e Great Gardens at
urhead *left* and the
se are now under the
e of the National Trust.
e gardens represent one
he 18th century's finest
dscape designs.

e great Elizabethan
nsion of Longleat is the
ne of the Marquess of
th. The park is one of
many that were
dscaped by Capability
wn. *Above* shows the
gnificent saloon and
't the equally
gnificent State Dining
om.

55

Edward I conferred the title
'Regis' on the medieval port
Dorset that is now known a:
Lyme Regis *left* when he
sheltered in its bay during hi
wars with the French. It bec
one of the first seaside resor
the south-west during the 18
century and its popularity h:
increased with the years.

Shaftesbury *centre left* was :
fortified town in Saxon time
overlooks, and provides
magnificent views of, the
Blackmoor Vale and it figur
Thomas Hardy's novels und
old name of Shaston.

The huge figure cut into a
hillside *below* near Weymou
variously known as the
Osmington Man, or King
George III.

Westwards from the popula:
tourist spot of Lulworth star
the huge limestone arch of
Durdle Door and the magnif
Man o' War Bay *left*. The tru
majesty of Durdle Door may
be seen from the beach on a
day, when the sea crashes
through the arch – a truly
awesome and elemental sigh
Another view of the beautif
coast near Lulworth is show
overleaf.

Corfe Castle *right* is one of t
most spectacular of all Brita
ruined castles. During the C:
War it was a Royalist strongl
that held out long after most
the others had succumbed. C
it fell, however, it was largel
destroyed, many of its stone:
going to provide building
materials for houses in the
village.

58

A popular yachting cen[tre]
Lymington *left* lies on t[he]
Lymington River near t[he]
edge of the New Forest [in]
Hampshire. From Pier
Station car ferries leave
for the Isle of Wight,
across the Solent. The
great seaport of Portsmo[uth]
is another popular
departure and arrival po[rt]
for passenger and car
ferries *below right* linki[ng]
the mainland with the I[sle]
of Wight.

Winchester was already
an important town in th[e]
times of the Romans an[d]
became the Anglo-Saxo[n]
capital, remaining so un[til]
the reign of William the
Conqueror. Not surpris-
ingly, the city is full of
interesting buildings,
pride of place being
taken by the splendid
cathedral *below*. Parts o[f]
the original structure,
which was started in 107[9]
may still be seen and the
great Winchester Bible
dates from the 12th
century.

Bournemouth *above rig[ht]*
is a town par excellence
for the holiday-maker a[nd]
indeed, it was designed a[s]
such. Lewis Tregonwell
built a holiday home on
land here in 1810 and it
was from such a small
beginning that the 'Que[en]
of Resorts' as it is know[n]
today, grew. The town is
ideally situated as a
holiday resort; it faces
south, has a pleasant
climate and miles of
golden, sandy beaches.

61

Green, Hampshire
left is the perfect
g for a friendly game
cket. Situated near
hurst, it is an ideal
ng point for trips into
tractive woodland of
ew Forest.

ampton *left* has its
s deep in history. It
rom here that the
m Fathers set sail, in
on the first lap of their
ourney.

eace and tranquillity
English countryside is
nised in the picture
taken at Fullerton, on
ver Test.

ugh it lies within the
y of Hampshire, the
Wight is separated
mainland England by
aters of the Solent. The
of Godshill *right* lies
south of the island.

e idyllic scene *left* was taken
he lovely hamlet of Swan
een, which lies at the heart
he New Forest.

dlers Mill *top* was pictured
he old market town of
nsey.

difficult to imagine that
tiny village of Buckler's
rd *above* was once a great
building centre. In fact, the
memnon, Lord Nelson's
urite ship, was built there
781. In those days ships
e built of wood, and the
tiful oak in the nearby
w Forest made Buckler's
d a logical choice for the
ding of these magnificent
els.

ht. West Green House, now
he care of the National
st.

The Channel Islands are s
governing islands off the n
west coast of France that
belong to the British Crow
and were originally part o
old Duchy of Normandy. I
addition to being very pop
holiday islands they are
famous for two breeds of
cattle and the fruit, vegeta
and flowers that are grow
there.

The town church in St. Pe
Port, the capital of Guern:
shown *top left*, Creux harl
on the island of Sark, *bott
left*, and Portelet Beach an
the Ile au Guerdain, Jersey
right. The beautiful sunse
right was photographed a
Corbiere in Jersey.

The Isles of Scilly are a tin
group of islands that lie al
thirty miles south-west of
Land's End. The climate c
islands is mild and the ma
source of revenue for the
islanders, besides tourism
obtained from flower-gro
The Scillies' only town is
Town, on St. Mary's, the l
of the islands. *Centre left*
the Neptune Steps in the
Tresco Gardens.

The Isle of Man is set in th
Irish Sea. One of the smal
independent sovereign
countries under the Crow
has its own Parliament, th
Tynwald, which administ
own laws and raises taxes
'Lady Isabella' at Laxey, *a
is the world's largest wate
wheel.

67

834 the Duke of
vonshire inherited a small
age on the south coast. He
berately set out to build a
l resort, albeit on different
s, from the nearby one of
ghton and in so doing he
ated Eastbourne, Sussex
, which has increased in
size and popularity whilst
retaining its intended
ance.

e Eastbourne, Brighton
an as a small fishing
nlet. George III's son, the
nce of Wales, became
nce Regent in the early part
he 19th century and
aged John Nash to enlarge
old pavilion into the
ravagant structure *bottom*
that we see today. Largely
ause of the Prince's
rest, Brighton became the
ntry's leading resort and
ains one of them to this

e Long Man of Wilmington
ove is believed to have been
by the Saxons.

achy Head *top right* and its
hthouse *centre right* are
matic sights, no matter
w often they are seen. Each
ange in the weather
nditions, no matter how
otle, adds a different
nension to the view; it is as
ually as impressive in bad
ather as in good.

ling Gap *right* is a cleft in
South Downs, and lies
ween the mouth of the
ckmere River and Beachy
ad.

stbourne's esplanade *ove*, with its colourful wer beds, skirts the sea nt and leads towards e magnificent chalk adland of Beachy Head.

e Armoury, Winchelsea *ove left*. Winchelsea s built by Edward I to place the old town that d been submerged by e encroaching sea. It nds on a hill opposite, d rivals in beauty and arm, Rye *right*.

st Dean *left* lies in the ley of the River Lavant. nsisting of flint and lf-timbered houses, it is ypical and charming wnland village.

Rye, Sussex *left* is
acknowledged to be one of
the most picturesque town
in the whole of England.
Somehow it has managed t
keep its ancient charm whi
still catering for an ever-
increasing flow of visitors.
is essentially a town to wal
around, for most of the old
streets are cobbled and the
is something to see almost
every foot of the way. The
houses are a mixture of
medieval, Tudor, Stuart an
Georgian and where restor
ation has been necessary, t
has been done in keeping
with the original style. Tod
Rye is almost two miles
inland, but it was once righ
by the sea and was one of
the Cinque Ports. The
harbour silted up in the 16t
century and with that natu
disaster the prosperity of R
as a port, not surprisingly,
declined. One of the most
interesting of Rye's historic
buildings is the Ypres Tow
which was the original old
town fort, built in the 13th
century, when it was know
as Badding Tower.

The picture *below* was tak
near Lewes and it exemplif
the beauty of the South
Downs.

iet and peaceful
sham *right* has an
eresting history.
gend tells us that this
s the place where King
nute demonstrated to
courtiers that he was
 able, as they had
isted, to command the
 to roll back. In 1064
rold left from Bosham
the journey that led to
meeting with William
Normandy and his
parture is recorded in
 Bayeux Tapestry.

 Bluebell Railway
ow is run by the

ebell Railway
servation Society and
one of the very few
aining steam railways
in Britain.

 gentle, English
mer scene *centre*
t shows cricket being
ved at Patcham Green,
ghton.

 Woodman *right* is an
 near Arundel and it is
cal of many such
rming pubs in the
a.

The village of Headcorn in
Kent *left* is notable for its
timbered houses which
were used by immigrant
Flemish weavers in the 17th
century.

Situated on an island in the
middle of a lake, what
could be more romantic
than Scotney Castle *below
left*. Even the fact that it
is mostly in ruins adds to
the charm and
romanticism.

South of London, and not
far from Sevenoaks, is
Chevening Place *right*, the
country home of Prince
Charles.

The weather-boarded mill
centre right is at
Farningham, one of the
prettiest villages within
easy reach of London. It has

many 18th century houses
and the old manor house
was once the home of
Captain Bligh, of Mutiny on
the Bounty fame.

Westerham was the birth-
place of General James
Wolfe, victor of the Battle
of Quebec in 1759, during
which he was killed. His
statue *above* stands at the
head of the green,
dominating the main street.

Chilham *right* is one of the
least spoilt villages in Kent.
Only the keep of the
Norman castle remains, but
nearby is a very fine
Jacobean mansion and
many Tudor and Jacobean
houses.

overleaf. A fine view of
Canterbury Cathedral *right*
and the interior of the
Warrior's Chapel, in the
Cathedral *left*.

VETERI   FRONDESCIT   HONORE

THE BUFFS

...ldford's Guildhall
...*k left* was made by
...n Aylward in the late
... century. Guildford is
...end of the old and new,
...n the modernity of its
...edral to the old Angel
...el *centre right.*

...*ht.* The Market Place,
...gston upon Thames. A
...ving market town,
...gston upon Thames is
...eved to have been the
...onation place of at
...t six Saxon kings.

... village clock in
...nger Hammer features
...ith striking a bell
...*tom right.*

... Royal Coat of Arms
...*om* is a feature of one
...e entrance gates to
...v Gardens. Within the
...utiful gardens may be
...n the famous Chinese
...oda *below*, built in the
... century by Sir
...liam Chambers.

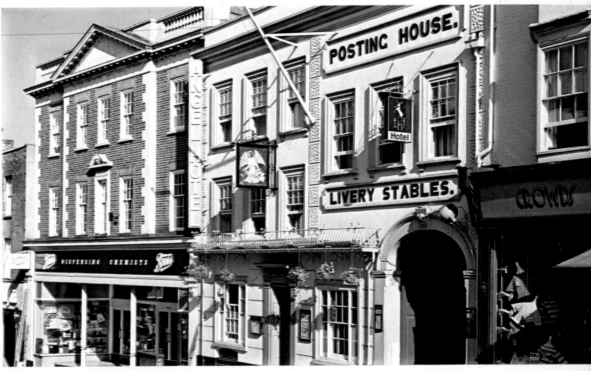

The attractive cottages *above* are at Outwood, Surrey. Nearby stands one of the oldest post-mills in the country. Dating from 1665, the mill still grinds flour, now only sold to visitors who come to watch the mill at work. Also in Outwood is the Bell Inn, pictured *bottom right*.

The West Course at Wentworth Golf Club *right*, near Virginia Water, is the scene of many notable golf tournaments.

Although Surrey houses an enormous commuter population it still retains much of its natural beauty. Sometimes, wandering through the countryside, it is almost impossible to believe that the great metropolis of London, with all its bustle and frantic activity, is only a few miles away. This, of course, is part of the county's attraction for people who spend their days in London; Surrey is such a pleasant place to come home to. The pictures shown *above and left* epitomise the quiet beauty that is to be found here.

81

Although Hampton Cou[rt]
Palace, which is picture[d]
on these pages, is closel[y]
connected with King
Henry VIII, it was not, i[n]
fact, built for him. It wa[s]
begun in 1514 and it was
originally the home of
Cardinal Wolsey. The
King was a frequent gue[st,]
however, and the palace
was eventually given to
him. A considerable par[t]
of the structure we see
today is original, but the
palace was enlarged and
improved by Sir
Christopher Wren duri[ng]
the reign of William III,
which time the facades
overlooking the garden[s]
were completed.

82

A view *below* of part of the lovely gardens and the Wren facade of Hampton Court Palace.

The British Isles are noted the world over for stately homes and palaces. Of these, there can surely be none more stately or famous than the Queen's home in Berkshire – Windsor Castle *right and above right*. Not far from London, it is within easy reach of visitors to the capital. The castle was originally built by William the Conqueror and lies in beautiful parkland on the banks of the River Thames.

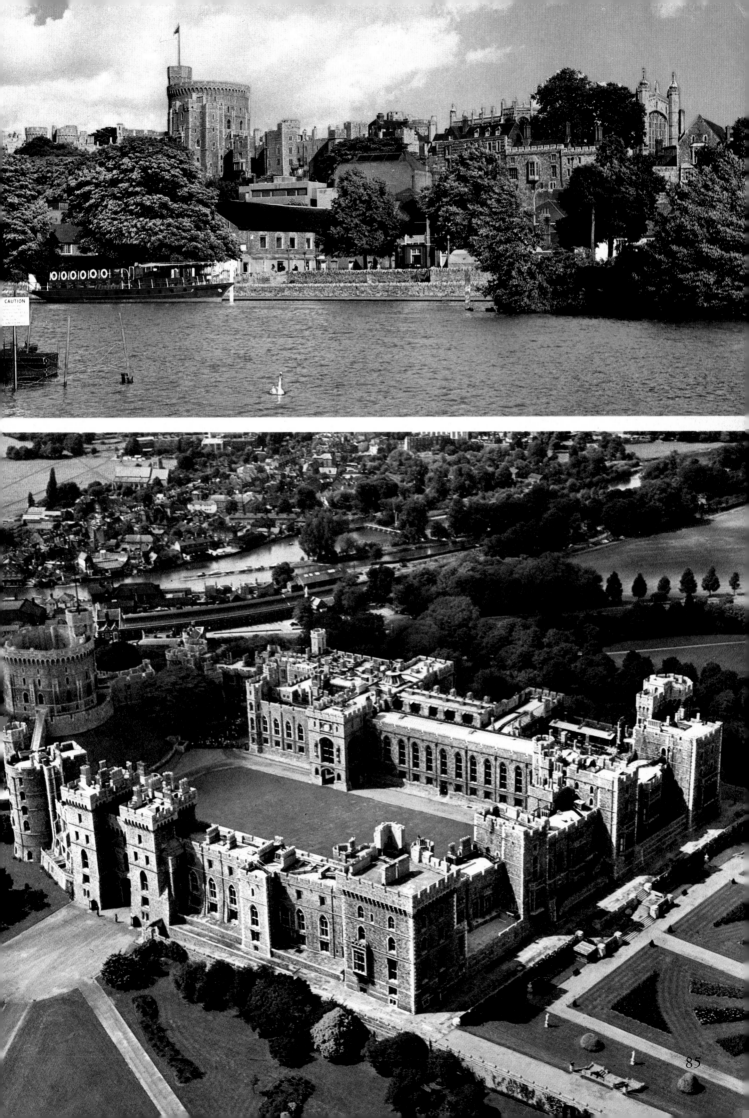

Windsor is famous, and
rightly, for its magnifice[nt]
castle, which contains
private apartments for [the]
Sovereign's use. The ca[stle]
right was founded by
William the Conqueror
and became a royal
residence during the re[ign]
of Henry I. During
successive reigns
additions were made to
the castle and much of i[t]
that can be seen from th[e]
river has been built sinc[e]
the 1820's. A guard outs[ide]
the State Apartments is
pictured *right*, and
Church Street, in the ol[d]
Victorian town, is show[n]
left and *bottom left*.

Across the Thames fro[m]
Windsor is Eton, famou[s]
for its College *above*
which lies at one end of
the quaint old High Str[eet].
Eton College was foun[ded]
by Henry VI in 1440, fro[m]
which time some of its
buildings date.

The Swan Inn *centre le[ft]*
at Streatley, which lies o[n]
the west bank of the Riv[er]
Thames, typifies the
unspoilt beauty of the
small town. From
Streatley Hill some of th[e]
finest possible views of
the Thames Valley may [be]
seen.

A university was first
established at Oxford in
the 13th century and, since
that time, it has become
one of the most important
centres of learning in the
British Isles, if not the
world. It has rightly been
called "a city of dreaming
spires' and it remains a
lovely city despite the
modernity that surrounds
it. It contains many
famous colleges and those
pictured here are:
Nuffield College *left*, St
Edmund Hall *centre left*,
the facade of St. John's
College *bottom left* and
All Souls College *below*.

The name Capability
Brown seems to crop up
whenever the great
gardens of stately homes
are mentioned and it was
he who created Blenheim
Park, near Woodstock,
damming the River Glyme
to make the lake. In the
park stands Blenheim
Palace *above right*, the
birthplace of Sir Winston
Churchill in 1874.

The regatta course at
Henley-on-Thames *right*.
It was in Henley, in 1839,
that the first river regatta
in the world was held. It
has now become a major
event, held every July. It
achieved its present title
of Henley Royal Regatta
in 1851, under the
patronage of the Prince
Consort.

Well-known for the world-famous regatta that is held there each year, Henley on Thames *right* lies in a lovely wooded part of the Thames Valley. The fine Georgian houses are particularly impressive, lending great dignity and character to the town.

The picturesque little village of Goring, where the lock *below right* was photographed, lies on the River Thames in a vale of the Chilterns, where the Icknield Way crosses the river on its long journey from East Anglia to the South West. In the belfry of Goring Church there is an ancient bell, cast in 1290.

Magdalen Tower and the Punters' Station, Oxford *above*. The old university town of Oxford is still dominated by the buildings and traditions that date from medieval times. On May morning a 17th century hymn is sung at the top of Magdalen Tower at sunrise and this is followed by a free-for-all on the punts – accompanied by a great deal of splashing and pushing-in.

91

It could be said that the Golden Age of Queen Elizabeth I began at Hatfield in Hertfordshire for it was in the great park here, in 155
that the young princess was told of her accession to the throne of England. A wing of the original Royal Palace still exists in the
delightful gardens of this Jacobean house *below*.

The old mill *above right*, at Hambleden in Buckinghamshire lies on the River Thames between Marlow and Henley, in the heart o
the boating country. The village of Hambleden has a 17th century manor house, a Georgian rectory, Roman remains in a small
museum and a fine church dating from 1633.

The peaceful and serene setting *right* belies the fact that the bustle of London is less than an hour away. Marlow has always been
popular with boating enthusiasts, situated as it is on one of the loveliest stretches of the Thames.

94

The pretty River Blackwater *above left* rises near the village of Seward's End and then meanders through the Essex countryside to Maldon, where it opens out into a wide estuary. It passes, on its journey, the silk-manufacturing town of Braintree and the lace-making village of Coggeshall.

Epping Forest *left*, with its 5,600 acres of beautiful woodland scenery, is a quiet haven not twenty miles from the great metropolis of London. The forest has belonged to the City of London since 1863. South of the town of Epping stands Waltham Abbey, dating from 1556, where King Harold, killed at the Battle of Hastings, is buried.

Finchingfield *above*, one of the prettiest villages in Essex, has many interesting houses and cottages. The church is also of note, being Norman in origin with the tower still remaining. An old post-mill still stands in the village.

As well as being an important farming area Suffolk is a county of great beauty. It was at time an important wool trading centre and, as is usual in areas where tra has prospered, a great of the money made by wealthy merchants wa spent on fine houses ar churches. With the dec of the wool trade many the merchants moved away, but they left the countryside greatly enriched.

Suffolk was the hom of John Constable, certainly one of, if not greatest of England's m fine landscape painters He interpreted the landscape that he saw around him in a fresh, way, and his paintings, particular the many co 'impressions' that he sketched were to prov inspiration to the new school of Impressionis that followed.

Constable was born the village of East Bergholt and the River Stour and its banks provided the subjects many of his most famo works.

Walsham le Willows *to left* is a village of weat boarded and timber-framed houses and cottages set in the hea tree-rich parkland.

A typically English vil Cavendish *centre left* a village green with thatched cottages and Church of St. Mary clustered around it. Su Ryder has established of her homes for refug from all parts of the w in the 16th century rec

The village of Kersey *bottom left* must be or the most photographe all Suffolk's villages. T is no wonder, for it is certainly one of the m picturesque.

Norwich, Norfolk, once
centre of the wool trade,
city of great history. The
cathedral *above* dates fr
the 12th century and the
is full of fascinating old
buildings such as
Tombeland Alley *above*
right.

Horning *left and right* li
on the River Bure betwe
Wroxham and Acle and
an extremely popular
centre for angling and
smooth-water sailing *fa*
right.

99

Although the county of
Norfolk is famed, and rig
so, for its excellent
waterways it has, in add
to the Broads, a great de
interest to offer. Picture
left are the ruins of Cast
Acre and *centre left* is
Sheringham, a fishing po
and seaside resort some
miles west of Cromer.
Bottom left shows Potte
Heigham, on the Norfol
Broads.

Great Yarmouth is anot
of Norfolk's popular hol
resorts. It contains a
fascinating model villag
below which is always a
great favourite, particula
with children.

The magnificent cathed
right at Lincoln dates fr
the 11th century and in i
soaring central tower ha
'Great Tom of Lincoln'-
bell weighing 5½ tons.
Within the cathedral th
are many fine examples
wood-carving, and the l
of the four copies of the
Magna Carta is also hou
here.

Queen's Gardens, King
upon-Hull, Humberside
above right. A famous p
with extensive docks, H
a centre of Great Britai
fishing industry. The cit
strong associations with
William Wilberforce an
statue overlooks Queer
Gardens.

Cambridgeshire is a coun[ty] of fine buildings such as Ely Cathedral *below*. The jewel of the county, however, is surely Cambridge, the famous seat of learning set on the banks of the River Cam. Beautiful lawns sweep down to the river *below right* on which punts mak[e] their lazy and peaceful way, passing under bridge[s] that are reminiscent of Venice, in particular the Bridge of Sighs *overleaf left*.

Top left is a view of the lovely Christ's College an[d] *centre left* is 'Nevilles Court', Trinity College, a college that is also feature[d] *overleaf right*. King's College is shown *left and above right*.

102

The lovingly-tended grav
in the American Cemete
in Cambridgeshire *left* a
those of American
servicemen who lost thei
lives in operations agains
the enemy during the
second world war. The vi
above shows the
cemetery's Memorial
interior.

The cathedral city of
Leicester is built on the s
of Ratae Coritanorum, a
old Roman settlement, a
there are still traces of th
Roman occupation in th
city. The Gothic Clock
Tower *above right* dates
from 1868 and *right* is th
old East Gate of the city.

great period of canal
struction took place
ing the 18th century
by 1830 there were
re than 4,000 miles of
igable waterways.
ove left is shown the
and Union Canal and
k at Braunston,
rthamptonshire.

tsworth House *left,*
rbyshire, is the seat of
Duke of Devonshire. It
ads in its own deer
ks which are watered
he River Derwent.

nded in 1881,
ttingham's University
lege moved from its
jinal site to the Trent
lding, University Park
ve, in 1928.
ttingham, famous for
associations with the
law Robin Hood, is an
University town with
ny interesting buildings
uding the Council
use *right,* which houses
Lord Mayor's Parlour
the Banqueting
oms.

The Royal Shakespeare
Theatre *left* at Stratford
upon-Avon, Warwicksh
was opened in 1932 and
replaces the theatre tha
was destroyed by fire in
1925. The town of
Stratford is renowned,
of course, as the
birthplace of Shakespea
below right in 1564.

The medieval fortress of
Warwick Castle *below* i
perched on a crag above
the river Avon, over-
looking the grounds
originally laid out by
Capability Brown.

The thatched and
timbered cottages of
Welford-on-Avon *right*
typify the rural England
that is so close to the
hearts of millions of
people throughout the
world.

ere can surely be no figure in
erature more revered than
lliam Shakespeare and his
thplace in Stratford-upon-
on has become a shrine for
rary pilgrims from all over the
rld.

ove left. The Royal
akespeare Theatre seen across
e River Avon.

ne Hathaway's cottage in
ottery, *left and overleaf* was
r home until her marriage to
lliam Shakespeare in about
2.

veral members of
akespeare's family, including
great man himself, are buried
he lovely Holy Trinity Church
ove.

mpton Wynyates *right* is a
utiful Tudor manor house
t was the home of the
mptons even before the
ning of Magna Carta.

e famous church *top* at
rwick dates from the 14th
tury.

113

7th century garden
trees *left* in the
n of Packwood
e are a symbolic
sentation of the
on on the Mount.

s House *above* and
Place foundations,
ord.

rick has, in addition
mposing castle, a
h of interesting and
esque old buildings
was in Warwick
he photograph *right*
dge End was taken.

117

Some of the loveliest countryside in England is to be found in Staffordshire. The view *above far left* shows the Roaches from Hen Clouds, near Leek.

Caer Caradoc Hill *left* lies about two miles north-east of Church Stretton. Halfway down the hill, on the western side, is the cave where Caractacus, the British chieftain, made his last stand against the Romans in AD 50.

Coventry, in the West Midlands, is a city with many historic associations. One of the most famous is the story of Lady Godiva *above left* and her ride through the streets, 'clad only in chastity'. The unfortunate 'Peeping Tom' is also commemorated by an effigy overlooking Hertford Street.

Above right is pictured the Bull Ring in Birmingham, West Midlands, which, with its modern buildings and bright neon signs contrasts vividly with the older areas of the city.

Cheshire is noted for its
fine examples of half-tim
architecture. Swans glid
idly on the moat comple
the grace and charm of I
Moreton Hall *above*.

Left is the Cross, at Ches
where unique galleried s
still exist in the heart of t
notably well-preserved c

Bramall Hall *right* date
from the 16th century an
acknowledged to be one
the finest examples of th
half-timbered style in th
country.

Chester's lovely red sandstone cathedral *right* was originally designed as a Benedictine Abbey, with monks' living quarters around the cloisters. Mainly 14th century, the building was a powerful monastery until after the Dissolution, when it became a cathedral and Bishopric. There is an important addition to the cathedral building complex, namely the free-standing Bell Tower, which was designed by George Pace and opened in 1975. It stands near the east end of the cathedral and is a concrete structure with a Bethesda slate cladding.

Blackpool is dominated by the 518 ft Tower *below*. This famous and extremely popular seaside resort on the north-west coast of England attracts many millions of visitors each year during the holiday season. The lighting of Blackpool's extensive and magnificent illuminations is a tradition that is eagerly awaited each year.

The setting of Liverpool Docks *overleaf, above right and right* belies its importance as a busy and essential link in the import and export of goods from and to all parts of the world. Liverpool is also noted for its university, fine cathedrals and art galleries. The Royal Liver building in the distance in the top picture oversees the manoeuvring tugs in the foreground.

124

Liverpool's Roman Catholic Cathedral *left* was designed by Sir Frederick Gibberd and building began in 1933. The original design, by Sir Edwin Lutyens, was for a quite different style of building but the outbreak of war, increasing costs and changing tastes in architecture were all responsible for the modifications that eventually produced the present cathedral which was consecrated in 1967.

One of the showpieces of Manchester is the Perpendicular Gothic cathedral *above*. It was formerly the parish church and is notable for its tower and the particularly fine woodwork it contains. Considerable rebuilding has been necessary since the 15th century, including the removal of the side chapels, and this has resulted in the cathedral having a particularly wide nave.

The Lake District encompasses some of the most beautiful countryside that the British Isles have to offer. The district is a mountainous one which includes such lakes as Windermere, Ullswater and Derwentwater but this is only to state the obvious and in no way conjures up the beauty and majesty of the Lake District through all the seasons and in all its moods.

The picture *left* was taken from 'Low Bank' and the beech trees *below* with their light dusting of snow were pictured at Ullswater which, at seven miles long, is one of the longest of the lakes.

Right. Snow at Kentmere in Cumbria. Kentmere is a village only a few miles east of Lake Windermere in an area that is famous for the beauty of its fells.

The most isolated of all the lakes is Haweswater *overleaf.*

Coleridge, Southey and Wordsworth have often been described as 'Lake Poets' and Wordsworth almost certainly saw his "Host of golden daffodil – fluttering and dancing the breeze" whilst walki around Rydal Water or Grasmere, near his Lake District home. The who area of the Lake Distric has been the inspiration many poets, writers, painters and photo-graphers and it continue to be so.

The pictures on these pages show just a small sample of the delights th await the visitor to the Lake District.

Tarn Hows *top left* is the result of the damming th turned three lakes into one in the early part of this century.

'Ruskin's View' over the Lune Valley *centre left* from Kirkby Lonsdale.

The Langdale Pikes *left* are in what is now the Lake District National Park, and *above* is a typical Lake District far

Grange Fell *above right* showing the view lookir towards Grange, in Borrowdale, and Fellsid *right*, near Keswick.

133

Snow, particularly fresh
snow, transforms all
things. Whilst it would
necessarily be true to sa
that snow beautifies the
Lake District it certainl
transforms the landscap

Long Sleddale *left* is a
long, sheltered valley. N
the most easily accessib
part of the Lake Distric
is nevertheless one of th
most rewarding for the
tranquillity it offers.

Below is the picturesqu
Ashness Bridge, Derwer
Water, with Skiddaw
rising behind it.

Watendlath *right* lies
south of Derwent Wate
and it was the setting fo
Sir Hugh Walpole's nov
Rogue Herries.

The beautiful area of England which is known as the Lake District has provided the inspiration for writers, poets and artists through the years.

Hartbeck *above left* is near Patterdale, at the head of Ullswater.

Watendlath *left* is situated in a hanging valley of the Derwent near the so-called Devil's Punchbowl.

Winter brings new contrasts and textures to the green mountains and blue waters of Tarn Hows *above*.

It was on the shores of Ullswater *right* that the poet Wordsworth saw the daffodils that inspired him to write his famous poem.

137

Rievaulx Abbey *left* was founded by the Cistercians in 1131. At one time it housed 140 monks and no less than 500 lay brothers, but by the time of the Dissolution parts of it had already fallen into disuse. Many people consider the ruins to be one of the loveliest sites in England.

To lovers of English history the city of York is a mecca. Medieval walls built on Roman foundations, timber-framed houses almost meeting overhead in the old Shambles, a wealth of old churches, such as St. Mary's Abbey *below* each with a history to be absorbed and, of course, the glorious Minster *right* which has been called, with justification a 'poem in stone'.

Fountains Abbey *top left*
was founded in the 12th
century and took three
centuries to complete.
Bolton Abbey *above* date
from the 13th century. It
stands on the River
Wharfe in what is now
part of the Yorkshire
Dales National Park.

Aysgarth Falls *left* form
part of the tortuous River
Ure. It flows through the
pastoral beauty of
Wensleydale.

The picture *above right*
shows how well the River
Nidd enhances the beauty
of the delightfully situated
town of Knaresborough.

Whitby *right* is a
picturesque red-tiled
fishing town that has
many associations with
the explorer, Captain
Cook.

141

...uker *left* is in the Upper-
...aledale area of
...rkshire, among the fells
...d moors that are so
...ch a feature of this part
...the country.

...e typical scene *below*
...t is of the countryside at
...alham, in the most
...gged part of the county
...Yorkshire. Nearby is the
...agnificent Malham
...ve, a spectacular
...nestone amphitheatre
...eated by movement of
...e earth's crust during
...e Ice Age.

...e Shambles *right* are
...rrow, medieval streets
...York that now house all
...nner of interesting
...ops but they take their
...me from the Old
...glish *shamel*, meaning
...ughterhouse, for this
...s the original purpose
...the area.

...iew of York taken at
...ht *above* from the city
...lls.

...e industrial shot *centre*
...ht is of Middlesbrough,
...Cleveland, on the Tees
...uary.

...eds town hall, *below*
...ht, centred in Victoria
...uare is a highly
...ccessful architectural
...ample of 'classic' revival.
...was built in the 1850's
...d opened by Queen
...ctoria. Since the
...dustrial Revolution
...eds has continued to
...ge ahead and indeed
...mains the ready-to-wear
...thing capital of the
...untry.

e of the finest Norman
dings in England,
ham Cathedral *above*
stands high and fortress-
above the River Wear.
ing from about the same
od are the ruins *left* of
nard Castle which was
uilt by John Baliol,
estor of the founder of
iol College, Oxford.

nstanburgh Castle *right*
begun in 1313 by the
of Lancaster and was
subject of several
ous paintings by Turner.

rian's Wall *above* is
bably the most famous
e of Roman Britain. The
of the wall was to
ect the frontier of
e's province of Britain
nst invasion from the
es to the north. It was
tually abandoned in
383.

Lindisfarne Castle, Holy Island, Northumberland *below*. A brooding sky seems to emphasise the defensive aspect of the castle, perched on its steep rock. The island, some three miles long by three-quarters of a mile wide, can only be reached at low tide, but it is well worth a visit in order to see the ruins of the early Benedictine Abbey.

Overlooking the Northumberland coast, Dunstanburgh Castle *right* presides over an area that has been officially declared one of outstanding natural beauty. The ruins of the 16th century castle changed hands no less than five times during the Wars of the Roses.

Newcastle upon Tyne *right* is a well-known port and industrial city in Tyne and Wear that is noted for the manufacture of armaments and ships and is also famous for its coal. Newcastle was the point where the Tyne was bridged by the Romans and it was known, in those days, as Pons Aelii.

146

Wales

Some of the most impressive scenery in the whole of Great Britain can be found in Wales: land of magnificent mountains and gentle valleys, charming mountain streams and. cascading waterfalls, spectacular passes, remote, wood-fringed lakes, green undulating hills and heather-clad moors.

The backbone of Wales, and the heart of the magnificent scenery, is the Cambrian mountains, and Mount Snowdon at 3560 ft is the highest mountain in Great Britain south of the Scottish border. From Roman times Snowdonia has attracted climbers eager to accept the challenge of the rugged and dangerous rock faces and in the 18th and 19th centuries artists were frequent visitors, inspired by the breathtaking landscapes which remain unspoilt today.

The Cambrian mountains, together with the Brecon Beacons and the Black Mountains, form an integral part of Welsh history. For centuries they acted as an effective barrier against invaders, but in turn the Romans, Normans and Plantagenets broke through, all eager to rule the strong-willed Celtic inhabitants of this relatively isolated part of Britain. These different cultures left their individual marks on Wales: the Romans built roads and fortresses and the legionary camp at Carleon, Gwent; the Normans built the solid castles of Chepstow and Pembroke and the Plantagenets built the fine castles of Caernarvon, Beaumaris and Harlech, under the direction of King Edward I. It was he who established English rule over Wales for the first time, in 1282-4. His son, who was born at Caernarvon, was created the first Prince of Wales, in 1301.

The beauty of Wales lies not only in its mountains and valleys. The county of Dyfed, south-west Wales, has a dramatic, weather-beaten coastline, with high cliffs and sandy bays. Delightful resorts such as Tenby and St David's make it a favoured holiday area. St David's, named after the patron saint of Wales, is the smallest cathedral city in Britain.

In south-east Dyfed lies the town of Carmarthen, which is said to have been the birthplace of the legendary wizard, Merlin. It was believed that he cast a spell on an oak tree in Priory Street, declaring that if it should ever fall, so would the town. Such is the strength of legend that the rotting stump can be seen today, embedded in concrete and supported by iron bands!

One of the most attractive towns in Dyfed is undoubtedly Laugharne, with its old castle and picturesque harbour. It was here that the famous Welsh poet, Dylan Thomas, lived for many years. Several of his poems were written in the tiny, remote cottage by the waterside, overlooking the magnificent hills, and it is the town of Laugharne and its inhabitants on which "Under Milk Wood" is believed to have been based.

Off the coast are several craggy islands which are inhabited only by vast numbers of seabirds and seals. Grassholme Island, just 12 miles offshore, is one of the largest gannetries in the world, with more than 15,000 pairs of gannets nesting there.

A characteristic of the northern part of Dyfed is the extensive, sweeping moorlands and the magnificent coastline. The River Teifi is a haven for salmon and trout anglers and the art of fishing from coracles is still practised. These tub-shaped boats have been used since the time of the Ancient Britons and except for canvas in place of hide to cover the wicker frames, the design has remained unchanged. There is little industry in this area but many of the traditional crafts, such as weaving and woodcarving, prosper here as well as in other parts of the country.

Industry developed mostly in Glamorgan, and has left its mark on the once green and peaceful valleys of the Brecon Beacons. Pontypridd, Neath and Rhondda are the locations of the numerous unsightly iron and coal mines that have given employment to many in the last 150 years whilst resulting in the destruction of much of the surrounding beauty. Today, however, work is being done to recover the scarred country-side by the clearing of tips and planting of trees.

The largest city in Glamorgan and the capital of Wales since 1955 is Cardiff, the great seaport on the Bristol Channel. It rose to prosperity with the building of the first dock in 1839 and the subsequent export of coal. Today it is a modern industrial city with many docks and factories. Its large stadium, Cardiff Arms Park, is the Mecca for supporters of Welsh rugby football.

In common with many of the counties of Wales, Glamorgan has numerous lovely beaches, particularly between Barry and Porthcawl. The Gower peninsula, too, is a restful retreat from the industrial suburbs, and here the cockle gatherers of Penclawdd can be seen, driving their ponies and donkeys across the treacherous sands of the silted-up Loughor Estuary, to the prized cockle-beds.

Bounded on the south by the Bristol Channel and to the east by England, is the county of Gwent. It was here that Caractacus and his Silurian tribes fought against the invading Romans. In later years the Normans, struggling hard to maintain control over this border country, constructed stalwart castles. Although in ruins today, Chepstow Castle still commands an impressive position over the River Wye and the medieval streets of the old market town. Close by are the remains of Tintern Abbey, a monastery founded by the Cistercian order of monks who were suppressed by Henry VIII in 1536. The Abbey has been described as the jewel of the Wye valley, so outstanding is its setting, and has been the source of much artistic inspiration for both painters and poets.

Now a part of the larger region of Powys, the old county of Radnor, characterised by its large expanses of moorland and isolated hills, was so sparsely populated that sheep outnumbered people. The area is known for its old spa towns, such as Builth Wells and Llangammarch Wells and its reservoirs provide soft, Welsh water for Birmingham.

The bustling town of Welshpool, in the north-east of Powys, is renowned for its outstanding Georgian architecture. The showpiece of the town, however, is Powys Castle, built in 1250. The gardens were formulated in the 18th century by the celebrated Capability Brown, and include a 181 ft high Douglas Fir, which is reputedly the tallest tree in Britain.

One of the areas most frequented by holiday makers is the northern coast of Wales. The large resorts of Colwyn Bay, Llandudno and Rhyl and the smaller ones on the pretty island of Anglesey are popular for sunbathing and swimming, especially with people from nearby Merseyside, and there are plenty of places of interest to visit in the beautiful surrounding countryside should the sun not shine.

The Welsh people's intense pride in their country and language is nowhere better illustrated than in the many Eisteddfods that are staged every year. Their love of singing and dancing, and writing and speaking their musical language, reaches out to inspire all who go to watch and listen.

Conwy Castle, Gwynedd, North Wales, *left.*

The county of Gwynedd
covers an area of the no[rth]
west tip of Wales and
includes the isle of
Anglesey. Notable amo[ng]
the many beauties of th[e]
county is the attractive
resort of Conwy *above.*
easily does Telford's
suspension bridge blen[d]
with Conwy Castle *righ[t]*
that it is difficult to ima[gine]
that six centuries elapse[d]
between their construc[tion.]

The famous Snowdon
Mountain Railway *left* [runs]
during the summer mon[ths]
from Llanberis up the s[teep]
barren mountainside to [the]
summit of Snowdon, at
3,560 feet the highest
mountain in England a[nd]
Wales.

The renowned 679 feet
high Great Orme's Hea[d]
overlooks the beautiful
sweep of Llandudno Ba[y]
above right, with its fin[e]
beach and good bathing

150

The beach scene *above left* was taken at Morfa Nefyn, on the Lleyn Peninsula. *Left* is Traeth Bychan on the low-lying island of Anglesey which is also the setting for South Stack lighthouse *above*. The island is linked to the mainland of Wales by Telford's magnificent suspension bridge *right*.

Overleaf. Llanberis Pass showing Llyn Peris and Llyn Padarn.

153

The design of Caernarvo
Castle with its different
coloured masonry has
suggested a resemblance
the walls of Constantino
and the idea has been pu
forward that Edward I
intended it to form a visi
link with the old Welsh
legend that holds that th
was the birthplace of the
Emperor Constantine. Tl
castle, which stands on tl
Menai Strait facing
Anglesey, was the
birthplace of Edward, so
of Edward I, who was
destined to become the
Prince of Wales. The mos
recent investiture was, of
course, that of Prince
Charles in 1969.

LLANFAIRPWLLGWYNGYLLGOGERYCHWYRNDROBWYLL-LLANTYSILIOGOGOGOCH
RAILWAY STATION

e smallest house in
tain, *left*, has two tiny
ms and a staircase, a
ns. frontage and is
ins. high. Built in the
century, this once
erman's cottage is
d on Conwy Quay,
ynedd.

e longest station sign
Britain *above* is now
sed in the museum at
rhyn Castle. Mercifully
rtened to Llanfair P.G.,
n the romantic
ning of "The church
t. Mary by the hollow
vhite aspen, over the
rlpool and St. Tysilio's
rch close to the red
e" would have
founded the most
eterate train traveller.

e narrow gauge
stiniog Railway Station
t, set in the magnificent
e slate quarry region,
s originally built to
ry the slate from the
rries to Portmadoc. It
s reopened for
sengers in 1954 and
s from Portmadoc to
uallt.

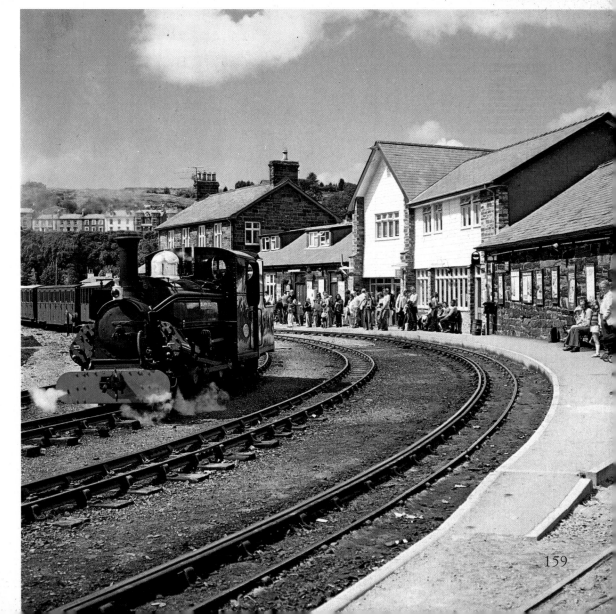

159

160

gellau, Gwynedd *left,*
in a long valley and is a
ular centre for touring
Vales including, perhaps,
sit to the Barmouth and
wddach Estuary, *below*
Barmouth is a popular
day resort with fine
ds and excellent bathing
ities. There are also
utiful beaches and safe
ing at Benlech *right* on
east coast of Anglesey.

Italian village of
tofino inspired the
sh architect Clough
iams-Ellis to create a
m in stone –
tmeirion *below.* Many
ure films have been
e using this unique
ge as a location.

161

A shepherd, with only his dogs for company, drives his sheep *left* through the wet, green bracken of a leafy lane at Dolgoch, near Towyn, deep in the Cader Idris mountain country.

The beautiful Afon Mawddach *below* rises on the slopes of the 2,901 ft. Aran Benllyn, and flows down through the wonderful Snowdonia National Park to the sea at Barmouth Bay.

An unusual way of visiting Tal-y-llyn *right and overleaf* in the summer is by the Tal-y-llyn Railway which is the oldest steam hauled narrow gauge passenger railway in the world.

Harlech Castle *below right* was completed by Edward in the 13th century. It was the last stronghold of the Lancastrians in North Wales and also the last held by the Royalists in the Civil War.

162

as Newydd, Llangollen, Clwyd *left*. This beautiful 18th century mansion was the home of the Honourable Sarah Ponsonby and dy Eleanor Butler, who were affectionately known as the 'Ladies of Llangollen'.

short distance from the market town of Llangollen is the aptly-named Horseshoe Pass *below left,* which rises to a height of 1,300 ft. om here there are excellent views of the fine scenery in the area.

The ruggedness of the Eglwyseg Mountains, Llangollen *above* belies the softer pastoral qualities of the lovely vale that they shelter. This is one of the major beauty spots of Wales and attracts many visitors each year.

The Pool and Craig Ddu *overleaf* pictured from the mountain road that leads to and from Aberystwyth in Dyfed.

The wonderful Dyfed co
from Carmarthen Bay to
Cardigan Bay provides s
quite magnificent scener
left, as well as some very
attractive little cliff-top
villages such as Tresaith
right, which lies some mi
south-west of New Quay

Autumn tints set off the
splendour of the Furnac
Falls *below,* one of the m
picturesque scenes that t
part of the country has to
offer.

Aberaeron *below right* is
splendid little holiday sp
ideally situated at the mo
of the Afon Aeron. The
surrounding countryside
particularly beautiful an
the lovely Vale of Aeron
attracts many visitors.

guard *above left* is a
resque fishing village
ed high above the old
ur. This small port and
also a holiday resort
g fine cliff views and
ng from a shingly beach.

roke Castle's walls *left*
erly encircled the town
he remaining parts give
wn a romantic, and
st medieval, appearance.

traggling town of St.
d's is dominated by its
dral *above*. St. David's is
n's smallest cathedral city
radition tells us that St.
d, the patron saint of
s, founded a church and
astery on this site.

harming holiday resort of
right is situated on a
sula at the west end of the
n, where a lighthouse
s the entrance to the
ry.

The City Hall, Cardiff *le*
Cardiff is the capital of
Wales and an important
port on the Bristol
Channel as well as a
University City. The cas*
below dates from Norm*
times and was once the
home of the Bute family
was built on the site of a
Roman fortress and has
been altered many times
throughout the years.

Although parts of
Caerphilly Castle *right* ar*
in ruins it still remains an
imposing fortress. The
town grew up around the*
castle and its markets
were renowned for the
excellent Caerphilly
cheese that was sold ther*

The Mumbles Lighthous*
below right, on the east
coast of the Gower
Peninsula, stands on
Mumbles Head, guardin*
the entrance to Swansea
Bay.

ruins of the 12th to 14th
...ury Cistercian Abbey
...ve left at Tintern, in
...ent, stand in a romantic
...ded setting by a curve of
...River Wye.

...siderable remains of the
...priory at Llanthony,
...ent, still stand in a
...ghtful part of the Vale of
...as left.

...Brecon Beacons
...onal Park, where the
...ure of the sunlight
...kling on lingering ice
...snow above was taken,
...nds over an area of
...e than 500 square miles
...includes the snow-
...red peak of Pen-y-Fan
...which reaches a height
...906 feet.

Scotland

To the north of Stirling Castle stand rank upon rank of ancient mountains, providing some of the most magnificent scenery in the British Isles. These are the Highlands of Scotland, a haven of pine woods, purple heather moors, peaceful lochs and sparkling streams. Away from the main centres of population, this area attracts many thousands of visitors eager to experience a more tranquil way of life and to enjoy a wealth of unspoiled countryside.

The coastline of the Western Highlands resembles the rugged fjord coast of Norway, with long fingers of water reaching far inland. Offshore are the Inner Hebrides, a chain of islands that provide calm waters for small sailing boats. On the small island of Iona St Columba established his abbey in the 6th century and St Oran's cemetery, the oldest Christian cemetery in Scotland, is the burial-place of many Scottish Kings. The romantic island of Skye is the largest in the Inner Hebrides – rich in legend and historic relics. Bonnie Prince Charlie was a welcome fugitive there after his escape from the English at the Battle of Culloden in 1746.

Farther west are the Outer Hebrides. Here, fishing plays an important role in the lives of the islanders. Stornoway, on Lewis, is the largest town and the centre of the high quality Harris Tweed industry. Much of the weaving of this excellent and popular cloth is still done in the home but spinning and finishing is now carried out in modern mills on the island.

The Shetlands and the Orkneys, groups of islands to the north, were settled by Norsemen in the 9th century and remained under the jurisdiction of Norway and Denmark for five hundred years. Fishing and farming have been the traditional occupations for centuries but now, with the discovery of oil in the area, the way of life of the people of these islands is undergoing great changes. It is to be earnestly hoped that the wild and beautiful scenery will not be permanently marred.

Many of the Scottish islands are sanctuaries for numerous, and often rare, species of sea birds. On the mainland are to be found golden eagles, wildcats and deer, and glittering salmon and trout abound in the lochs and rivers. For the active holiday-maker, the Cairngorms, Glenshee and Glencoe are the principal skiing centres in the British Isles, providing facilities that can be favourably compared with resorts on the continent.

In the northern part of the Highlands the population is fairly isolated, living in sturdy crofts or in picturesque fishing villages. Farther south there are large towns such as Inverness – the gateway to the North West – close to the mysterious Loch Ness and at the eastern end of the Caledonian Canal.

Aberdeen, Scotland's third largest city, is built almost entirely of granite and it is an important centre for the fishing industry on the east coast. The seaport of Dundee, on the Firth of Tay, was the scene of many battles for Scottish Independence. It is also remembered for the disaster of 1879, when the Tay Bridge collapsed during a gale. Sadly, a train was crossing the bridge at the time and there was considerable loss of life.

The massive castle at Stirling, already mentioned, looks south to the site of the Battle of Bannockburn and to the Lowlands of Scotland. Here, the landscape is a gentler one of rolling, grassy hills and green valleys, where farming is less of a struggle and where nearly all of the country's industry is situated.

There are still delightful lochs such as Loch Lomond, which reaches a depth of 630 feet at its deepest point and is dotted with small islands, which attracted Irish missionaries in the 15th century as being secure places for their monasteries and nunneries. The haunting song 'Loch Lomond' is said to have been composed by one of Bonnie Prince Charlie's captured followers, on the eve of his execution, as he lay in Carlisle jail.

One of the greatest attractions of the Lowlands is the Border Country. This is a land separated from England by the Cheviot Hills, a land of majestic ruined abbeys and outstanding scenery that provided the inspiration for many of the novels of Sir Walter Scott.

Within easy distance of the industrial area of Clydeside are the pleasant seaside resorts of the Strathclyde coast as well as several internationally famous golf courses like Troon and Turnberry. Robert Burns, Scotland's national poet, was born at Alloway, just outside Ayr, on January 25th 1759, a date celebrated each year by Scotsmen all over the world.

Two thirds of the country's population live in the Lowlands, concentrated mainly in the two large cities of Glasgow and Edinburgh. Glasgow developed in the 17th century as a major port handling the sugar, cotton and tobacco that was being brought in from the New World. Additional prosperity came with the advent of the Industrial Revolution, when heavy engineering works and shipbuilding yards grew up along the banks of the vital River Clyde. Glasgow is today Scotland's largest city, but its growth has brought with it the attendant problems of overcrowding. It also, however, possesses a fine medieval cathedral, several well laid out parks, two great football teams and, not far away, some particularly lovely countryside.

Scotland's beautiful capital, Edinburgh, is dominated by its thousand year old castle that sits solidly upon a towering crag, some 443 feet high. East from this great landmark runs the Royal Mile, a name given to the ancient streets lined with many tall, 17th century buildings, which extends to the Palace of Holyroodhouse. Overlooking the palace is Arthur's Seat, an imposing, extinct volcanic peak that affords splendid views across the city.

Edinburgh's cosmopolitan atmosphere is nowhere better reflected than at the Edinburgh Festival of Music and Drama that is held annually. The participants include some of the world's most distinguished actors and musicians, who perform in front of over 100,000 visitors.

These visitors, and the many more who travel to Scotland each year, are always sure of a warm welcome. With so much beauty, history and so many fascinating customs, the people of Scotland are only too happy to share their proud heritage.

Pipers at Edinburgh Castle *left.*

e harbour and Girvan
boat *above right* set a
tty scene to welcome
tors to this popular
t fishing resort, which
tuated on part of
tland's most dramatic
stline, close to
nedy's Pass.

e Mull of Galloway
, in Wigtownshire, a
rious promontory,
nds in this half-
gotten corner of
tland, enjoying a
tle climate, thanks to
Gulf Stream which
s the cliffs and sandy
ches.

tpatrick *below right*,
he north of the Mull,
s once a "Gretna
een" for the Irish, who
uld sail the 21 miles
m Donaghadee in
thern Ireland, and after
ding on Saturday,
ring their banns read
Sunday, were married
Monday. The steamers
ssed the channel until
9, when silting and
s despoiled the
bour.

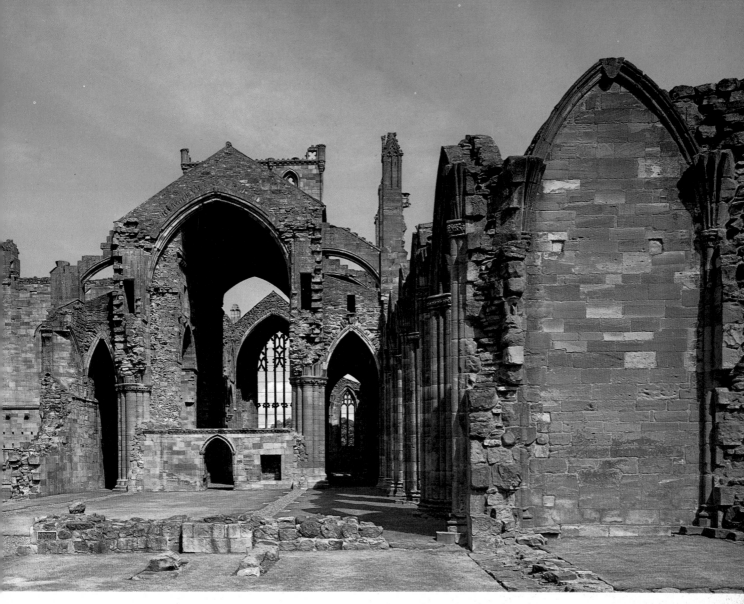

e Border hills have a
cination derived from a
tory of ballads, legends
d scenic charm. The Grey
re's Tail, near Moffat in
Dumfries and Galloway
gions, is shown *above*

mfries has many
ociations with the poet
ert Burns, who spent
last few years of his life
re. One of his favourite
lks was along the banks
he River Nith *left*
ards the ruined abbey
Lincluden.

utiful Melrose Abbey
ve is one of the prime
actions of the Borders
ion of Scotland. It has
ny associations with
ttish royalty and the
rt of Robert the Bruce is
ied beneath the high
r.

o in the Borders Region
bbotsford House *right*,
last home of Sir Walter
tt, who died here in
2.

Whether it is reached by high road or low, Loch Lomond *below* never fails to reward the traveller with unforgettable views. Renowned in story and song, it is the largest loch in Scotland and blends together in one scene all the unmistakable characteristics of the Scottish countryside.

The 'Fair City' of Perth stands on the banks of the River Tay, in the Tayside Region, and was formerly the capital of Scotland. The peaceful setting *above right* belies the rich and sometimes violent history that the city has known and today Perth is the obvious choice for visitors who want to explore the Central Highlands.

Stirling Castle *right* still appears to stand guard over the surrounding countryside, although the days of siege that it has known are long ago.

The beautiful city of
Edinburgh is Scotland's
capital. Unlike most of
Britain's cities, which w
built alongside rivers,
Edinburgh was built on
crags. The city is full of
notable buildings and
famous streets, such as
Fettes College *left*, one o
the great British public
schools, and the Scott
Monument and Garden
Princes Street *below*. Th
busy thoroughfare of
Princes Street is also
featured *below right*,
dominated by the famou
castle, the origins of whi
are lost in time. Viewed
from the castle walls are
of the capital's best-kno
buildings *right*, the Roya
Scottish Academy and,
beside it, the National
Gallery of Scotland.

Overleaf: The Ross
Fountain in Edinburgh.

The bagpipe is an ancient instrument that was once played throughout Europe. Although it is still heard in several other countries, the instrument is now, in the minds of most people, a particularly Scottish one. The distinctive wailing music it produces can be sad or rousing and must surely be a heart-tugging sound to many thousands of expatriate Scots all over the world.

The pipers shown *above right* were photographed at the Royal Scottish Academy Exhibition and *right* at Edinburgh Castle. *Far left* is a member of the Royal Scots Dragoon Guards, and the piper *left* was pictured in Glencoe.

Top. The Royal Scots Greys Memorial in Edinburgh.

190

The Palace of
Holyroodhouse, Edinbu[rgh]
above, and seen from
Calton Hill *left*, stands a[t]
the foot of the Canonga[te].
Originally started by
James IV, most of the
present day structure,
however, was built for
Charles II. Here was
enacted one of history's
most famous murders w[hen]
Rizzio, the close friend [of]
Mary, Queen of Scots, w[as]
brutally killed before he[r]
by command of her
husband, Lord Darnley.
Still, today, one of the
Queen's Official
Residences, the State
Apartments contain ma[ny]
treasures.

John Knox's house in th[e]
Royal Mile, Edinburgh
right, is now preserved [a]
museum. The Protestan[t]
Reformer was reputed t[o]
have lived here during t[he]
15th century, when he le[d]
the Reformation in
Scotland.

Overleaf. One of the gr[eat]
thoroughfares of the w[orld]
Princes Street from
Edinburgh Castle.

192

193

Night views of Edinburgh *left and below left.*

The Edinburgh Military Tattoo *above* takes place at Edinburgh Castle. The Tattoo evolved from displays of military drill during the 1948 Edinburgh International Festival and it has since become a very popular item on the programme. Although several units from overseas have taken part, the programme is mainly filled by British bands and display units.

The setting sun reflected in the water shows the Forth Bridges *overleaf* rather in the manner of an oriental painting. Both the railway bridge, in the foreground, and the recent road suspension bridge, beyond, are staggering feats of engineering, spanning distances between six and nine thousand feet.

The magnificent River
Clyde *left*, with its imme
docks and extensive
shipbuilding industry, is
world famous. The city o
Glasgow *right* has grow
and expanded over the p
150 years and is Scotland
largest city and seaport.

Lyle Hill, Greenock, affo
magnificent views of the
Firth of Clyde *below lef*
The famous Cross of
Lorraine was erected on
Lyle Hill in memory of t
Free French sailors who
died in the Atlantic duri
the second world war.

The view *below right* sh
the two bridges spannin
the River Forth. This
particular view was take
from South Queensferry

Connecting Loch Fyne a
the Firth of Clyde with t
Western Isles, the Crinar
Canal *above* is in an area
great natural beauty. The
canal was opened in 180.
although it was not final
completed until 1817.

The bulk of the Great
Shepherd of Etive *left*
dominates this view of o
of Scotland's most
impressive glens.

Oban *above right* is fine
situated on the shores of
picturesque bay in the
Strathclyde Region. Oba
a popular summer resor
the sheltered bay provid
beautiful views of sunse
amid the mountains of N

Sheltered in a narrow in
of Loch Fyne, Terbert *ri*
is a busy fishing port as
as a holiday resort.

Sunset over Loch Linnh
and Corran *overleaf.*

args, in Strathclyde *left*, was the scene of a decisive battle between the forces of Alexander III and the King of Norway in 1263. The wn looks across the Clyde to Cowal, Bute and the Isle of Arran.

he lovely sunset *below left* shows the fragmentary remains of Dunure Castle. Dunure is a popular holiday resort and fishing village.

Much changed since the days of the poet, Ayr is a natural choice of starting point for a tour of Burns Country. From the harbour *above* the seaward view is impressive and beyond the bulk of Ailsa Craig it is possible to discern the Irish coastline.

The beautiful sunset *overleaf* features Kilchurn Castle, Loch Awe, in the Strathclyde Region.

Buachaille Etive, Glen
Etive, in Argyllshire
above, is one of the
magnificent sea lochs ir
this rugged, western
coastline, rich in
mountain grandeur.

Head of Glencoe, with
"Sisters", Aonach Eagac
left, presides dramatica
over one of Scotland's
most celebrated glens.

Still in Northern
Argyllshire the beautif
River Beathach in Glen
Orchy *above right* refle
in the still waters, the
isolation of this
wilderness.

Inveraray Castle,
headquarters of the
Campbell Clan since th
15th century *right,*
faces Loch Fyne and is
surrounded by some of
loveliest woods in
Scotland. A five mile w
leads to the derelict ho
of the legendary Rob R
whose dirk handle and
sporran can be seen on
display in the castle.

The village of Ardgour is
situated on the western
shores of Loch Linnhe
above. The snow-covered
mountains provide a per[ ]
backdrop to the calm bl[ ]
waters of the loch.

Bordered by the old road[ ]
Glencoe, the shores of L[ ]
Tulla *left* are noted for t[ ]
relics of the pines of the
great Caledonian Forest[ ]

Standing on a tiny islet i[ ]
Loch Laich, off Loch
Linnhe, Castle Stalker
above right looks onto a[ ]
region familiar to reade[ ]
Robert Louis Stevenson[ ]
'Kidnapped'.

Part of the Inner Hebrid[ ]
the Isle of Mull guards t[ ]
entrance *right* to Loch
Linnhe and is separated
from the mainland by th[ ]
Sound of Mull to the no[ ]
and the Firth of Lorne t[ ]
south. The undulating
scenery of the island is
notably picturesque.

212

Beautiful Easdale in
Strathclyde *left* is typical
of this part of Scotland's
scenery.

Robert Burns, Scotland's
most celebrated bard,
commemorated by this
Statue in Ayr *below*,
can justly be called the
"Poet of Humanity". The
Monument and River
Doon *centre left* is seen
from the Brig O' Doon.
The simple, arched bridg
which still spans the rive
reminds one of "Tam
O' Shanter", in which
poem it was mentioned.

Oban *left*, surrounded by
string of castles, is truly t
great port for the Wester
Isles; centre of Gaelic
culture and Gateway to
the Mull.

The Harbour and Dunba
Castle *right*, now lying in
ruins, once sheltered the
tragic Mary, Queen of
Scots, before she finally
surrendered to her
insurgent nobles in the
16th century.

Pittenweem *left*, situated in the Kingdom of Fife, home of Scotland's Kings from Malcolm III until the Union of the Crowns, is a picturesque coastal resort whose fishing fleet can be seen *right*. Fife's greatest fame, however, is probably as the home of golf, played at St Andrews for at least 500 years and brought to Scotland by the traders of Holland.

The 'Study' and Cross Culross, Fife *below,* has been excellently maintained by the National Trust for Scotland, although only the choir of the 13th century Abbey remains. The enchanting cobbled streets of Culross' carefully preserved 16th and 17th century town, with its red-tiled houses, are a joy to behold.

217

Old houses frame the busy harbour of Pittenween *right*, which has been a Royal Burgh since the days of Scotland's David I. This is a part of Fife once notorious for its witches, and as late as 1746 a woman was sentenced as a practiser of unholy arts. The imposing church tower, which resembles that of a castle, dates from 1592.

Crail *above and right* is a very old and picturesque fishing town in the east Neuk of Fife and it has many buildings dating from the 16th century. The church, partly 13th century, is of considerable interest, as are some of the ancient carved memorials in the churchyard. Of particular charm are the old crow-stepped, and red-tiled, houses near the harbour.

The Royal and Ancient Golf Club of St Andrews was founded in 1754, and today it is the foremost in the world. Golf is believed to have been played here in the 15th century. The picture *right* shows the famous Road Hole, the seventeenth, on the Old Course.

Above and right: The Cathedral ruins, St Andrews, Fife. Built staunchly facing the cold North Sea, St Andrews seems braced for more than just the elements. Such inflammatory matters as golf rules, John Knox's sermons and modern students' polemics are in the tradition of the town. The cathedral was founded in 1160 and it is just one of the many fascinating places to visit.

221

Glen Clova *left* leads in
the heart of the Grampi
Mountains. This area is
extremely popular with
hill walkers although th
views from the road
circling the glen are
equally rewarding.

Glamis Castle *below*
stands in fine grounds
bordered by the Dean
Water. It is one of the m
notable buildings of its
period in Scotland and i
reputedly haunted.

Dundee, essentially a
modern city with
extensive docks along t
Firth of Tay, has importa
engineering and
shipbuilding industries.
Dundee *below right* the
River Tay is bridged in t
places. The famous rail
bridge, dating from 1883
carries the main line fro
Edinburgh to Aberdeen
and the new road bridge
right, completed in 196
replaces the old car ferr
to Newport-on-Tay.

South-west of Perth lies
the world-famous golf
course of Gleneagles *le[*
The setting is superb,
matched only by the
quality of golf that
Gleneagles has witness[

In the heart of the
Trossachs lies the Port [
Menteith *left centre*, a ti[
resort, nestling on the la[
from where visitors can
take the ferry to visit
Inchmahome and wand[
through the remains of [
13th century Augustinia[
Priory, once a retreat fo[
tragic Mary, Queen of
Scots.

Balquidder on Loch Vo[
above is steeped in
romance, since here lies
buried the infamous Ro[
Roy, whose exploits and
tales of derring-do, have
surely fired the
imagination of countles[
boys all over the world.

The glinting sun filterin[
through the russet leave[
brings Autumn to Loch
Tummel *left*. Here one [
imagine Queen Victoria
standing on the north
bank, now aptly named
Queen's View, being
enchanted by the vista
which lay before her.
The nodding daffodils
bring Springtime to
Aberfeldy *right* and bid
joyous welcome to this
pretty market town wit[
its five-arched stone
bridge over the River Ta[

Ben Lawers overlooks the large and deep Loch Tay *left*, noted for its salmon fishing. The mountain is the highest in the region and is of particular botanical interest.

Kinnoull Hill *below*, east of Perth, rises to a height 729 feet and is a magnificent vantage point affording fine views of the River Tay and the 'Fair City' as well as the beautiful surrounding countryside.

The road from the lovely village of Strathyre to Callander winds along the eastern shores of Loch Lubnaig *right*.

Lying on the fringe of the beautiful wooded Trossachs district, Loch Katrine *below right* is one of the loveliest lochs in Scotland.

228

The fishing vessels are moored and the nets are left drying in the picturesque harbour of Gourdon *left*. The coastline along this part of the Grampian Region is extremely rocky, but the harbour and village of Gourdon are sheltered by Doolie Ness.

High on a rocky headland the ancient ruins of Dunottar *below left* stand vigil over the North Sea.

The splendour of snow-clad Lochnagar makes an impressive backcloth for the Old Bridge of Dee *right* at Invercauld.

Although in ruins the magnificence of Elgin Cathedral *below*, as it once was, is still apparent. Founded in 124 by Bishop Andrew of Moray, the cathedral was considered "inferior to few in Europe".

229

To the east of the flat-topped Cairngorms lies the beautiful Valley of the Avon *left* where winter sports alternate with angling to make it an all-year resort.

Tucked in the lee of the red cliffs of Gamrie Bay in the Grampian Region is the secluded fishing village of Crovie *right*.

Macduff, opposite the town of Banff on Banff Bay, is an important fishing town with a large harbour *below* to accommodate the fleet of fishing vessels that puts out to sea each day.

Situated on a rocky part of the coast on the eastern side of Spey Bay is the village of Findochty *below right* with a harbour which is a natural attraction to visitors of all ages.

BF.10   OCEAN-HARVEST

Although still a fishing po[rt]
and the home of deep-sea
trawlers, Aberdeen
harbour *right and below
right* is now a busy base
for vessels concerned wit[h]
the relatively new North
Sea Oil operations.

The charters of Aberdee[n]
left and below date back
to 1179. Today it presents
remarkably clean and
solid picture, being built
largely of granite, and it i[s]
often referred to as 'The
Granite City'.

232

234

erdeen *left and below*
is Scotland's third
gest city, and has been
sely associated with
bert the Bruce since
ose far away times when
rallied his men against
Comyns, rival
ntenders for the
ottish Crown, with his
of "Bon Accord". Built
ost entirely of local
nite, this fine city owes
ch of its present day
osperity to the fishing
dustry.

e tranquil Loch Unagin
ht, in Inverness-shire, is
ked to the magnificent
ledonian Canal, an
tstanding engineering
sterpiece of the 19th
tury. The canal itself
s along the Great Glen,
nnecting several lochs,
uding Loch Linnhe
t centre, where the
ely King George V can
seen sailing through.

nfinnan, a tiny hamlet
e head of Loch Shiel,
re the Prince Charles
ward Monument looks
dramatically over the
above, is a fitting
nder that on this spot,
he 19th August, 1745,
nie Prince Charlie
ed his father's standard.

e midst of the Central
hlands, the snow
ed mountains of
tonmore *right,* with
r sugar icing topping,
e the wild and desolate
ery which is a
ominant feature of
part of Scotland.

...uhart Castle *left,* in the
...hland Region, stands on
...shores of Loch Ness. Its
...s form one of the most
...uresque views of the
...a. The elusive Loch Ness
...ster was first referred to
...quitalis Bestia' in the
...century.

...rness Castle *below left*
...rds magnificent views of
...surrounding Highland
...ery. It was built on the
...of a former stronghold
...royed by Bonnie Prince
...rlie during the '45
...llion.

...dling in the richly-
...ded Strath Spey, which
...des the Cairngorm and
...nadhliath mountains,
...more *right* is a popular
...hland winter sports
...rt which also offers
...d climbing and walking
...ntry.

...end has it that the
...cess who built Castle
...l *below* on the Isle of
...e stretched a chain
...ss the strait – or kyle –
...kin, in order to extract a
...from ships wishing to
...s. The magic scenery of
...e, the Misty Island,
...pts one to believe such
...s without question.

237

r many people,
vernesshire is
nonymous with the
ghlands, the picture-
stcard part of Scotland,
ich is never more so
an when covered in
ck snow. Tulloch
llage *right*, nestling in
ft white drifts, is a
pical example; whilst
low in Glen Nevis, one
the loveliest of all the
ghland glens, the sturdy
ghland cattle brave the
nter landscape.

n Nevis, towering over
rt William, *right centre*,
Britain's highest
untain, standing 4,406
high. Although
chanting under snow,
e mountain's
ecipitous northern flank
iims many
experienced climbers
ery year.

mortalised in song,
llaig Harbour *left*, the
mposer's "Road to the
es", is today a large
ring port. From here
itors may take the ferry
Portree on the
endary Isle of Skye,
eped in 4,000 years of
es of magic and mystery
holding a rich store of
ics from a bygone age.

enfinnian Viaduct
ht, still and softly
shed in the winter
w, portrays a very
ferent scene from those
rm golden tones of
gust when the clans
lied for Bonnie Prince
arlie, at what was the
rt of his attempt to
over his father's lost
wn.

243

...and's lochs provide some of the
...outstandingly beautiful scenery
...found anywhere in the British
...The wooded appearance of
...Laggan *left* has been greatly
...ged due to work in connection
...the Lochaber Power Scheme.

...er brings an arctic hue to the
...donian Canal, which follows the
...e of the Great Glen. It is seen
...*e left* under the shadow of
...in's highest mountain, Ben
...s.

...a jewel on a cloak of mountain
...moorland, Loch Affric *above* lies
...e of the loveliest glens in
...and.

...Insh *right* is an enlargement of
...ast-flowing River Spey – which
...ted for its excellent salmon
...g.

...ets are invariably at their most
...essive when viewed across
...r. The beautiful photographs
...*eaf* are of Loch Arkaig *left* and
...Morlicj *right*.

241

243

On this forbidding north western thrust of mainland, jutting out into The Minch, Sutherland offers solitude to the traveller glad to shake of the city dust. Weather permitting he can take the Kyleakin Ferry *right* from Kylestrome to Unapool. Unapool.

The dramatic Eilean Donnan Castle *left*, standing on an island where the Lochs Duich, Alsh and Long combine, was built in 1220 by Alexander II of Scotland and in the 18th century was a Jacobite stronghold. In the early thirties the ruined castle was restored by the MacRae family, and now houses a museum and clan war memorial.

At the mouth of Loch Carron, Plockton *below left,* sets its face towards the craggy landscape of the grey mountains, standing lonely on the Applecross Peninsula.

Looking out over the Pentland Firth, on the most northerly tip of Britain, stands John O'Groats *right centre.* To the south lies Wick, an ancient Royal Burgh, whose large harbour can be seen *right.* The wild rugged sea has claimed the lives of many sailors and wreckage can often be seen strewn at the foot of the jagged cliffs. Three miles north-east, from the lighthouse at Noss Head, breathtaking views of the ruins of Castle Sinclair *above* are a delight.

It is thought that there is
treasure lying in the bay o[f]
Tobermory *above*, on the
Isle of Mull. On the isle it[self]
there is no need to search
however, for the treasure[s]
are all around, in the natu[ral]
charm of the town itself a[nd]
its attractive wooded sett[ing.]

On a sandy bay overlooki[ng]
the Firth of Clyde, Rothes[ay]
left is a popular resort no[t]
far from Glasgow, on the
Isle of Bute.

Lochranza Castle on the [Isle]
of Arran *above right*. Dat[ing]
from the 14th century, the
picturesque double-towe[r]
castle looks out over Loc[h]
Ranza, where Bruce is
believed to have landed
from Ireland in 1306.

The romantic Isle of Skye [is]
the setting for the
magnificent Cuillins *righ[t]*,
mountain range of serrat[ed]
peaks and wild corries.

Ireland

Ireland lies directly in the path of the rain-giving Westerlies and it is this that makes it the greenest country of the British Isles. Its plentiful rainfall has caused it to be known, very aptly, as the 'Emerald Isle', and the variety of scenery and relatively unpolluted atmosphere make it a favourite retreat for holidaymakers, especially as some of the Irish roads are among the least used in Europe. Indeed, despite political troubles, tourism continues to flourish, but without spoiling the natural amenities that are Ireland's heritage.

The unhurried and seemingly casual way of life extends throughout the country. The fish-filled lakes and rivers are a paradise for the enthusiastic angler, and the many beautiful golf courses are both challenging and scenically superb. Mountains and valleys are abundant and are popularly viewed at a leisurely pace, on horseback or from a gypsy caravan. The spectacular, wild and rocky Atlantic coastline has a unique splendour, contrasting vividly with the many other fine, sandy beaches that Ireland has to offer.

For the sporting spectator there are many interesting events to be seen. The Dublin Horse Show and the Irish Sweeps Derby are both well-known, but the intriguing games of hurling and Gaelic football should not be missed. Hurling is reputedly one of the world's fastest ball games and involves a leather ball, or sliotar, being hurled with a broad-based ash stick called a caman. In Gaelic football the ball can be handled or kicked and injuries are not considered a serious enough matter for the game to be stopped!

Ireland has few cities but numerous small towns and villages, each with its own legends and quaint customs and all offering traditional Irish hospitality.

For the lover of history, Ireland is rich in historic buildings and prehistoric remains, including numerous megaliths. These are huge tombs, pillars and stone circles dating from 2,000 years B.C., when they were built throughout the country.

Ireland has been invaded a number of times. The most notable and influential invasion was by the Gaels in the 3rd century B.C. They named their new territory Gaelic Island and established their own language. Gaelic Island was divided into Kingdoms, each ruler being subject to the High King. Near Dublin is the Royal Tara, the seat of the ancient kings and a famous landmark.

Another significant event in Irish history was the foundation of Christianity in 432 A.D. by St. Patrick, the Patron Saint. Centuries of great monastic fervour followed, and thousands of Irish men and women devoted themselves to the service of God by becoming monks and nuns, many of whom were sent to Britain and Europe as missionaries. In 800 A.D., however, the Vikings began their raids, plundering the monasteries, killing many of the inhabitants and burning buildings, but they did carry out a partial colonization of the country and they founded the city of Dublin. In time they were defeated by the English and the Normans and English Rule then, as now, was the subject of bitter controversy, often leading to fighting, and this seriously hampered the economic advance of the country.

Cork harbour was once the main departure point for emigrants to North America and nearby, at Cobh, is one of the oldest yacht clubs in the world. The famous Elizabethan sailor Sir Walter Raleigh lived at Youghal and it is said that he planted here the first potatoes that he brought back to Europe. Another esteemed man of Cork was William Penn, who founded Pennsylvania but spent his boyhood in the county.

West of Cork is County Kerry, the first part of Europe to be sighted by Charles Lindbergh on his epic solo Atlantic flight from New York to Paris in 1927. The coast here juts out into the ocean, forming gigantic headlands that can be viewed from the Ring of Kerry road that winds around these promontories. Inland are beautiful lakes and mountains, especially around Killarney, where there are landscapes that alter with every season but always remain awe-inspiring.

The county of Tipperary, made famous in song, is the home of the Rock of Cashel, Ireland's most imposing ecclesiastical ruin. It was here that St Patrick plucked a shamrock as he preached, thus giving Ireland its universally recognized emblem.

Drained by the River Shannon, and also facing the Atlantic, is the farming county of Limerick. Sharing this long river is neighbouring County Clare, where the Transatlantic airport of Shannon is situated. Near the airport is Bunratty Castle, well-known for the banquets, a 20th century feature of many Irish castles, that are held within its walls.

County Connacht is the last land before America and it is here that the Gaelic language has been best preserved. Its scenery includes many pretty, thatched cottages where the traditional crafts of knitting and weaving are carried out.

The lovely counties of Connemara and Galway are noted for their majestic mountains and clear bog streams – landscapes that have inspired many of Ireland's painters. Along these coasts large numbers of ships from the Spanish Armada were wrecked and countless treasures were lost forever.

Over all these picturesque counties is the capital, Dublin, a city with a cosmopolitan air. Its many fine buildings include a castle dating back to the 13th century and two impressive cathedrals. In the city is one of the world's largest breweries producing the incomparable Irish stout known the world over as Guinness.

Dublin's counterpart in Northern Ireland is Belfast, which owes much of its development to the Industrial Revolution. The early town, however, grew up around a castle built in 1177.

Northern Ireland is often referred to as Ulster, although it contains only six of the nine counties which make up that ancient Irish Province. It too has a wide variety of attractive scenery. There are lakes and moorlands – the latter providing peat for drying and subsequent burning, basalt cliffs, drumlins and hillocks left by the retreating Ice Cap which covered Ulster so long ago.

Much has been written of the Irish people in songs and poems, stories and plays, by their most talented writers including William Butler Yeats, James Joyce, the fiery Brenden Behan, the inimitable Oscar Wilde and, of course, George Bernard Shaw. The Irishman's wit and blarney is well known and his relaxed approach to living is the envy of many. It reflects, perhaps, the natural beauty that surrounds him – beauty that has remained unchanged for centuries – the beauty that is Ireland.

Left. A Jaunting car in the Killarney National Park, Eire.

Little more than a centur
ago Belfast was no more
than an obscure village.
Today it is a busy port and
one of the most importan
manufacturing cities in th
British Isles. The dignifie
Parliament House at
Stormont *above* stands ir
public park of some 300
acres. At the crossing of t
avenues is L.S. Merrifield
statue of Lord Carson.

Situated in beautiful
grounds, Belfast Castle *le*
was built by the 3rd Marc
of Donegal and dates fro
1870.

In University Street stand
the wonderful old Tudor
style building of Queen's
University *above right* w
its square tower. The
university was founded in
1849 and incorporates
excellent, up-to-date
teaching facilities.

The City Hall, Belfast, *rig*
is an impressive edifice
which was designed by
Cromwell Thomas and b
in 1906. The 173 ft. high
dome is topped by a light
and affords a magnificen
view of the city and
surrounding countryside

pretty harbour of Ballintoy
…ge *above left* looks out to
…hlin, the stocking-shape island
… is a stepping-stone to
…tland.

…w miles from the impressive
… formation of the Giant's
…seway is the picturesque
…ge of Dunseverick *left*.
…rby, on a steep-sided rock, are
…remains of the castle which
… destroyed by Cromwell's
…es.

…village of Bushmills *above*
… on the River Bush – which
…vides excellent fishing. It is
… far inland from the pleasant
…ch of Portballintrae.

…ite Rocks, Portrush *right*. The
…e Portrush is derived from
…Gaelic 'Port Rois' – meaning
…bour of the Headland – and
…town is indeed situated on the
…y Ramore Head, jutting
…st a mile out to sea.

253

nbane Castle *above left* stands
me three and a half miles
rth-west of Ballycastle. It was
ginally built by Colla
cDonnell in 1547 and is now in
e charge of the local County
uncil.

ne of the most picturesque
ins in Northern Ireland,
nluce Castle *left* is on the
ast, quite near the Giant's
useway. The castle was
cated in 1639 after the kitchen
nd the servants in it –
ddenly fell into the sea.

e coastal walks around the
lage of Ballintoy *above* are
ried and delightful and the
a is a favourite subject for
ists.

minating the coast five miles
st of Ballycastle is Fairhead, or
n More *right*. From here there
e excellent views across to
thlin Island and beyond to the
ast of Scotland.

The White Rocks near
Portrush *above left* are
where the surging waters
of the Atlantic meet the
North Channel of the Irish
Sea, and the action of the
waves has carved out the
fascinating caves and the
strange rock formations
left. On a clear day the
Mull of Kintyre in
Scotland can be seen from
here.

Carrickfergus, whose
castle and harbour are
pictured *above*, is a few
miles south of Larne, the
terminal of the shortest
sea route from Britain.
The castle was built by the
Normans and has been
restored to keep its
original 13th century
character.

Owned and cared for by
the National Trust, the
rocky islet of Carrick-a-
rede *right* towers 350 ft.
above the sea and is linked
to the mainland by the
famous rope bridge which
is only 84 ft. above the
waves.

257

The famous Mourne
Mountains *left*, rendered
immortal in song and vers
are the highest in Norther
Ireland. Dominated by
Slieve Donard, 2,796 ft.,
which rises to the south-
west of Newcastle, the
tallest peaks command
exceptional views.

The Hermit Bridge and
Falls, Newcastle *below*, a
in the Tollymore Forest
Park, one of the most
beautiful of the five fores
parks in Nothern Ireland.

The relatively modern
Bangor Castle *right* stand
the attractive Castle Park
the southern extremity of
the town.

Situated on the low-lying
Ards Peninsula, the famo
Ballycopeland Windmill
below right is one of the f
mills in existence in Irelan
It is believed to date from
16th century and has
wooden parts that are still
working order.

...rlinford Lough, Co.
...wn, *above left* is a long,
...rrow inlet of the Irish Sea
...t separates County Down '
...m the Irish Republic.

...r *left* are the famous
...untains of Mourne –
...owned for their natural
...uty.

...e three-storeyed square
...ver *left* of Narrow Water
...stle was built in the 16th
...ntury on the site of an
...lier stronghold. It stands
... a rocky promontory in
... Newry River estuary.

...amous port in the Middle
...es, Ardglass *above* is now
...entre of the herring
...ustry.

...keel *right*, the Church of
... Narrow, is an attractive
... prosperous resort with a
...utiful beach and busy
...ing and yachting
...bour.

261

Barnes Gap, Co. Tyrone, *left* famed for its lovely scenery, is a three-mile cleft through the mountains between the winding Glenelly and Owenkillew river valleys. This was once the land of highwaymen and kidnappers and the last wolf in Ireland was shot near here two centuries ago.

An elegant open space in the centre of Armagh, the Mall *above* is lined with Georgian houses, the work of the 18th century architect Francis Johnston.

Gortin Forest Park *left*. The charms and beauties of Ireland are many and varied and are seen to their best advantage in the popular forest parks.

Enniskillen, County Fermanagh, *above* is an ancient town on an island between Upper and Lower Lough Erne and the name means 'Island o Caitlin' – a legendary chieftainess.

To the south of Lough Erne, in the heart of the Irish lake district, stands Monea Castle *left* – a splendid example of the fortified homes built by the Scottish and English settlers.

Garrison is a fishing reso at the south-east end of the attractive Lough Melvin, where the lovely picture *above right* was taken.

Lough Erne *right* is a beautiful sheet of water, well-known to anglers ar popular with water sport enthusiasts.

265

The Guildhall, in Shipquay Street, Londonderry *below*, is an imposing building of Tudor-Gothic style with beautiful stained-glass windows. Shipquay Street leads from the centre of the old town to Shipquay Gate, one of the original gates of Derry.

Overlooking Magilligan Point with its old battery and martello tower guarding Lough Foyle, Binevenagh *above right* rises to 1,260 ft and commands fine views of the lough and the Inishowen Peninsula in Donegal.

An attractive seaside resort, Portstewart *right* has an Atlantic beach of more than two miles and two excellent golf courses. Although host to many pleasure sailing enthusiasts, Portstewart is also a main centre for deep sea fishing.

Dublin's famous Four
Courts *left* were begun i
1786. They were designe
by Thomas Cooley and
completed by James
Gandon and have a
frontage extending for
some 450 ft. The Custon
House *below* is
considered to be James
Gandon's masterpiece,
completed in 1791.

Below centre is O'Conn
Bridge, seen here at nigh
This, the finest of Dubli
bridges, is only one of th
many that link the north
part of the city with the
south.

Pictured *right* is
Castletown House, a
lovely Georgian house
that was built by Willia
Conolly, a speaker of th
Irish Parliament.

Bottom right. Coliemor
Harbour, Co. Dublin.

A view of Dublin City a
the River Liffey is show
overleaf.

269

Ardamine Strand, near
Courtown, Co. Wexford
left. Ardamine is a quiet
cove with an earthen
mound nearby which
covers a considerable are
and was probably some
form of sepulchre. The
nearby Courtown is a
seaside village with fine,
sandy beaches but the loc
fishing industry is greatly
hampered by silting-up o
the harbour.

The landscape *below* wa
taken in Co. Wexford, a
county that lies on Irelan
south-eastern coast.

The Round Tower at
Ardmore, Co. Waterford
right, was one of the last
be built in Ireland and is
particularly fine specime
It is divided into five stor
and stands approximatel
96 feet in height, with fou
windows in the top store
facing the cardinal point

...nestown, in County
...aterford *right,* is a
...all seaside resort on
...nbrattin Bay *right*
...ntre.* Nearby stands
...e ruined Dunhill
...stle, a ruined 17th
...ntury stronghold
...ich was the scene of
...avy fighting during
...e Cromwellian
...mpaigns.

...art from its
...clesiastical ruins and
... splendid tower,
...dmore is an excellent
...astal resort with fine,
...dy beaches *right.*

...e peaceful haymaking
...ne *overleaf* was
...ken near Kinsale, in
... Cork. The town
...elf has a long and
...eresting history and
... Multose's Church,
...ich dates back to the
...h century, is one of
...land's oldest parish
...rches.

Inchidoney Strand *left* overlooks the wide, secluded sweep of Clanikilty Bay. Shark fishing *below* is very much a feature of the area and there is a deep sea fishing centre at Kinsale, just along the coast.

The charming Italian gardens *right* are situated on Garinish Island in beautifully wooded surroundings at Glengarriff in County Cork.

Centre left is Ardrigole Harbour, West Cork and *left* is the lovely mountain lake called Gougane Barra, which is the source of the River Lee. High mountains rise around three sides of the lake and the whole beautiful scene is now a protected one, being contained within the boundaries of a National Park.

Bantry, Co. Cork *right*, is a small town in a hill setting with a fine harbour and good bathing beaches.

The view of Glanmore
Lough *left* was taken from
Healy Pass, one of the
finest of Ireland's
mountain roads.

Cahir Civeen *top right and
below left* seen from the
Ring of Kerry, the coastal
road that carries the
traveller around the shores
of the lovely Iveragh
Peninsula.

Slea Head *centre right*,
the roadside crucifix
above and the beautiful
coastal scene *right* were
all photographed on
Dingle Peninsula, a hilly
promontory extending far
out into the Atlantic
Ocean. Indeed, Dingle itself
is said to be the most
westerly town in Europe.

A cottage in the Kerry
mountains *above* and the
Gap of Dunloe, Co. Kerry
right.

Muchross Abbey,
Killarney, is shown *left*
and a thatched cottage
and ponies on the
Kenmare Estate *bottom
left*.

Below. A typical Jaunting
Car in Killarney.

Overleaf. The lovely,
secluded valley known as
the Glen of Aherlow,
Co. Tipperary.

The famous cliffs of Moher *above*, some four miles north-west of Lahinch, stretch along the pretty Atlantic coastline with its excellent sandy beaches.

Shoeing in the Forge at Bunratty Folk Park *left*. Here in his dusty environment the local blacksmith expertly plies his trade.

Cashel in Tipperary, steeped in history and famous for its rock, seen by night *above right*, owes its name to the stone fort which was erected on the summit in the 5th century. Hore Abbey *below far right* was founded in the 13th century by both the Cistercians and monks from Mellifont.

Standing in the cathedral doorway at Clonmacnoise, County Offaly *near right* one can watch the sun's last rays melt gently into the background, as gaunt O'Rourke's Tower fades into the night.

285

eve League, the
agnificent cliffs of Slieve
aght which dominate
e Inishowen Peninsula,
n be seen *above left*
wering almost 2,000 ft.
ove the sea.

shford Castle, near
ugh Corrib, in the
autiful County Mayo
ove, was once a
ansion belonging to the
uinness family and is
w a hotel.

unty Donegal, with its
cturesque glens and
nall lakes, is popular
ith many holiday-
akers and these
tractive cottages
ft offer idyllic
ccommodation.

ylemore Abbey *right*, an
apressive granite and
nestone building of the
th century, now
ccupied by nuns, is
tuated in one of the
veliest parts of Country
alway, by the shores of
llacappal Lough.

owerscourt Gardens
erleaf contain the
mous waterfall of the
me name.